What people are saying about

Welcome to the Rebellion

"In *Welcome to the Rebellion*, Harris explains how George Lucas' modern myth is rooted in radical political resistance against corporate authoritarianism with a message more relevant today than in the 1970s when it was conceived. He reveals the underlying political message of the *Star Wars* saga and its radical message which makes it more than a popcorn film, it's a document for resistance."
Jason Ward – Owner and Editor-in-chief of MakingStarWars.net

'For all of us who love *Star Wars*, for all of us who love humanity and our planet, for all of us who yearn to be part of the Rebel Alliance, this book is for you. Harris has given us this incredible resource to study, so that we can learn the ways of the Force, understand the very real and violent Empire of structural inequality and systems of supremacy we are up against today, and learn about the values and commitments of the also very real Rebel Alliance. Get this book, full of brilliant lessons and insights, study it, share it with others, and let it help us be the Rebels and Jedis for collective liberation that the world so desperately needs.'
Chris Crass – Author of *Towards Collective Liberation* and *Towards the "Other America,"* social justice educator and member of the Rebel Alliance

Welcome to The Rebellion

A New Hope in Radical Politics

Welcome to The Rebellion

A New Hope in Radical Politics

Michael Harris

Winchester, UK
Washington, USA

JOHN HUNT PUBLISHING

First published by Zero Books, 2020
Zero Books is an imprint of John Hunt Publishing Ltd., No. 3 East St., Alresford,
Hampshire SO24 9EE, UK
office@jhpbooks.com
www.johnhuntpublishing.com
www.zero-books.net

For distributor details and how to order please visit the 'Ordering' section on our website.

Text copyright: Michael Harris 2019
Cover image: Louie dela Cruz

ISBN: 978 1 78904 367 9
978 1 78904 368 6 (ebook)
Library of Congress Control Number: 2019905180

A CIP catalogue record for this book is available from the British Library.

Design: Stuart Davies

UK: Printed and bound by CPI Group (UK) Ltd, Croydon, CR0 4YY
US: Printed and bound by Thomson-Shore, 7300 West Joy Road, Dexter, MI 48130

We operate a distinctive and ethical publishing philosophy in
all areas of our business, from our global network of authors to
production and worldwide distribution.

Contents

Previous Titles

A Future for Planning: Taking Responsibility for Twenty-First Century Challenges (Abingdon: Routledge, 2019). ISBN: 9781138708808

Disclaimer

Neither this book nor its contents are endorsed or approved by or affiliated in any way with George Lucas, Lucasfilm Ltd., or The Walt Disney Company. The opinions contained herein are those of the author only. *Star Wars* is a registered trademark of Lucasfilm Ltd. and The Walt Disney Company.

Prologue: "The Rebellion Is Spreading, and I Want to Be on the Side I Believe In"

The deleted scene is in two parts and only lasts around 4 minutes in total, but it suggests a more radical *Star Wars* than we often recognize.[1]

It begins with Luke Skywalker in the Tatooine desert repairing a moisture vaporator.[2] He notices something high up in space. Through his binoculars he sees tiny glinting explosions. He rushes to Tosche Station in Anchorhead, where a group of young people are lounging around. Luke is surprised to find his best friend, Biggs Darklighter, and greets him warmly. Biggs is on leave from the Imperial Academy.[3]

Luke's friends follow him outside to see the battle, but it has already ended. Luke is ridiculed for imagining it. Biggs remarks that the Rebellion is a long way from here. One of the others doubts that the Empire would ever fight to save their system.

But in the second part of the scene, Biggs pulls Luke aside and shares a secret. He has "made some friends at the Academy." He is going to jump ship and defect to the Rebel Alliance. Luke almost explodes with excitement: "The Rebellion!?!" Biggs encourages his friend to come with him, but Luke can't. He has to help his aunt and uncle on their farm. Luke and Biggs part, hoping one day to meet again.[4]

The scene would have been intercut with the famous opening sequence in which a massive Star Destroyer chases down a Rebel blockade runner, stormtroopers blast their way onto the ship, and through the smoke steps the evil Darth Vader.[5] It was cut because it slowed the pace of the movie, but I knew this small bit of backstory since as a young fan I'd read the excellent 1976 novelization *Star Wars: From the Adventures of Luke Skywalker* ("Soon to be a spectacular motion picture from Twentieth Century Fox!"), ghost written by Alan Dean Foster.

1

The scene humanizes Luke earlier than in the released film. He's less a blank hero architype, more an awkward young man, torn between the chores of home and the call of heroism. A galactic civil war is raging, yet he can only watch from the sidelines.

But it also suggests that Luke and Biggs, and by implication many others across the galaxy, are more politicized than we might assume. Biggs explains that, "I'm not going to wait around for the Empire to draft me into service," a clear reference to the draft to serve in the war in Vietnam. As we'll see, *Star Wars* is very much informed by the protest movements of the 1960s. More than this, the saga is essentially a political story that continues to encompass today's conflicts.[6] Luke and Biggs don't seem like radicals, just regular young people, but this is clearly not the first time they've discussed rebelling: "It's what we always talked about, Luke."

Trying to persuade his friend to join him, Biggs emphasizes Imperial expansionism: "What good is your uncle's work if the Empire takes it over? You know they've already started to nationalize commerce in the central systems. It won't be long before your uncle's just a tenant, slaving for the greater glory of the Empire."[7] In the novelization, Biggs goes further: "You should have heard some of the stories I've heard, Luke, some of the outrages I've learned about. The Empire may have been great and beautiful at one time, but the people in charge now... it's rotten, Luke, rotten."[8]

Of course, the Empire does soon come for Luke, searching for two squabbling droids that are carrying secret plans for the ultimate weapon...

This book is about how a real empire of authoritarianism and corporate domination has now come for us. It rose to power within weakened and corrupted republics. It promised order and security, but relies on domination and fear, and now threatens our existence on a planetary scale.

But it's also about hope. Empire is more vulnerable than we often assume. The rebellion is all around us, and it is spreading. It is a struggle for freedom and democracy, and for peace and justice. In the face of multiplying crises, it is a rebellion that can no longer wait, and which will force us to take sides.

To win, we need to tell popular stories about the need to stand against empire. We need to believe that many more people are ready to join the rebellion than we are often told. And among other things, we need to claim popular culture to do it.

It means something that our most popular modern myth is a radical left story about fighting fascism. Contrary to postmodern cultural pessimism, the continuing popularity of stories such as *Star Wars* suggests the potential for a popular radical politics which is anti-authoritarian, pluralist, participatory, democratic and humane. From its roots in the 1960s new left, *Star Wars* still speaks to so many people today, including new generations of fans. It indicates a widespread desire to reject nihilism and despair, and to struggle against oppression and for liberation.

Yes, it's a space fantasy, but even so, go with it and the *Star Wars* saga can be used to illuminate the dark times in which we live. It also suggests that if we tell the right stories, we can welcome many more people to the rebellion and the fight for a better world.

Episode I

"Many of the Truths We Cling to Depend Greatly on Our Own Point of View"

"It's Not a Story the Jedi Would Tell You"

A rebellion is underway against elites and their greedy global order. It is amassing support from ordinary people, who feel marginalized and unheard. In a way they haven't felt for a long time, people feel an increasing sense of power and belonging. They are back at the center of the story, and elites fear them.

The problem is of course that they are part of a regressive revolt, a revolution led by the right: by Donald Trump in the United States, the hard Brexiteers in the UK, the hard right across Europe and autocrats across the world.

People are being conned. The programs and policies being driven through by the right will benefit only the already rich and powerful. Nonetheless, the story people have been told – of their subjugation and defeat, and their revolt and rise to victory – speaks to them. Our economic system increasingly says to people, "you are nobody." These stories tell people that they matter.

But how is it that such a story, which should naturally be owned by the left, has been seized by the right, and what do we need to do to reclaim the rebellion story?

Some might say that this demonstrates the inherent deceptiveness of stories, and people's credulity.[1] We need to counter stories with facts, re-assert notions of truth and disregard those who are prepared to believe what their own eyes should tell them isn't so. On its own, this would be a mistake; indeed, it is one the left has been making for some time. It has led to many defeats and much suffering. It is a mistake we have made because we don't believe in stories.

4

"What I Told You Was True...From a Certain Point of View"

Star Wars is about many of the things that we'll discuss in this book: freedom, democracy, oppression, exploitation, hope and rebellion. But the first thing *Star Wars* is about is stories and their power to shape politics.

The story that Obi-Wan Kenobi tells Luke about his father in *A New Hope* (a brave warrior betrayed by Darth Vader) is designed to set him on a path to joining the struggle against the Empire. It's a different story from the one Luke was told by his uncle to keep him toiling away on their homestead. In *The Empire Strikes Back*, Vader counters with yet another version of the story, actually the most accurate one, in an attempt to corrupt his increasingly powerful son. In *Return of the Jedi*, C-3PO uses his god-like status among the Ewoks to recount the story of the Rebellion and to recruit them in a military attack on an Imperial target. The whole of the prequel trilogy is really about the power of stories to manufacture chaos and confusion so that people accept authoritarianism. In *Revenge of the Sith*, Senator Palpatine/Darth Sidious tells Anakin Skywalker the tragedy of Darth Plagueis The Wise in order to manipulate him to the dark side. And *Star Wars* was originally conceived as a story within a story, an "historical" narrative taken from the Journal of the Whills, hence the famous 'A long time ago...' opening text.

None of these stories are the whole truth, but neither are they completely untrue. They all have truths in them, even when they are selective and told for a specific purpose. Similarly, the "rebellion versus elites" story that people have been told in our world may be fundamentally manipulative, but that doesn't mean it doesn't draw on what they have seen and experienced.

"Join Me, and Together We Can Rule the Galaxy Together"

It's the stories that engage and move people most that win,

especially when we feel anxious and afraid. As we'll see in later episodes, *Star Wars* is rather good at depicting how authoritarians use stories to serve their own ends. But these stories need time to take root, and they can't be created out of nothing.

For decades, in countries such as the US and UK, many people have seen their wages stagnate while the rich have got massively richer. They have seen their towns and cities decline, their hearts ripped out by globalization, outsourcing, automation and a lack of care. They have seen corrupt political elites doing the bidding of corporations. And they have been told a story of trickle-down economics which ended in a financial crisis, for which no-one was held accountable and which resulted only in austerity for the many.

It's not that, as often described in the mainstream media, people feel left out. They *are* left out. No wonder they were ready for a new story, wherever it came from, and they were willing, hungry, to shock the status quo.[2]

But the revolt from the right has its roots in a story that conservatives have been telling for a long time. Sociologist Arlie Hochschild describes the "deep story" that has been cultivated by the right for many years, of hardworking citizens struggling to get by while being bilked in taxes by a grasping government which privileges minorities and immigrants who "jump the queue."[3] As Steve Almond summarizes this "bad story": A government that seeks to redistribute wealth or curb greed is evil. Brown people are lazy and/or dangerous. White men are under assault. Elites and academics are mocking you. The mainstream media can't be trusted.[4]

This story was fairly easily adapted to the aftermath of the global financial crisis of 2007-2008. Although it was the bankers who were bailed out, conservatives directed the economic and cultural disenfranchisement they had stoked toward other, weaker targets. But as Hochschild suggests, it is not enough to blame Fox News and the Koch brothers: "[D]uping – and the presumption of gullibility – is too simple an idea."[5] A deep story of economic loss and cultural insult was lived long before Donald Trump descended his golden escalator. Trump appealed to the deep story, but he told it better than many other conservatives: about an American Dream lost to the country's "most deserving" and a duplicitous government that had sided with outsiders.[6]

Similarly, in the 2016 referendum on the UK's membership of the European Union, the Leave campaign's mantra of "Take Back Control" offered to reclaim power from unaccountable globalist elites and their national co-conspirators. It suggested that order and security could be re-established in an age of change and instability, and that ordinary people aren't as economically and politically irrelevant as they'd been told. On the other side, the Remain campaign offered an arid set of data based on the narrow, culturally-blind calculation that people ultimately only care about money. As with Trump versus Clinton, the side that told a story, a rebel story, won a shocking (but in hindsight, not so surprising) victory.

"He Was Deceived by a Lie...We All Were"

Much of the discussion, the agonizing, on the left and center-left has been about how all this happened, and the policies and programs necessary to respond to this revolt of the right. Important though these are, we also need to ask how the right has told better stories which reach more people. We need to take stories seriously – which is why we're talking *Star Wars*.

Senator Palpatine wouldn't have been able to take over the galaxy without telling stories, that's where his dark powers really lay. Similarly, the right understands that politics lies downstream from culture (Andrew Breitbart, the hard-right nationalist ideologue, said that), and culture is about stories. Perhaps it's also because the right, in terms of whose interests it serves, is inherently a minority. The fundamental challenge of right-wing politics is how to convince a majority of people that you are on their side when you aren't. For this, you need to tell stories.

Given that these stories will in reality provide nothing to ordinary people except further immiseration, the right is driven to double-down on a nationalistic identity-based politics. Indeed, in many ways the culture war has now become the near-totality of conservative politics (as we'll see, this even plays out around *Star Wars*), to the extent that the right's lapse into conspiracies and its rejection of facts suggests that it is being eaten by its own stories.

Despite this, or perhaps because of it, far-right parties are seizing power across Europe, in Austria, Italy, Poland, Germany, Slovenia, the Netherlands and France – and are not just aiming at older voters but preying on the young, for example the racist Identitarian movement (we'll return to the lure of the authoritarian right in a later episode).

However manipulative, the stories these groups tell are clearly effective. They draw on the behavior and self-interest of politicians, domineering corporate interests and the hopelessness felt in forgotten people and places. Not only do these stories identify the problems and the villains, they cast ordinary people as overmatched heroes: regular folk doing battle against mendacious elites. They allow people to see themselves as rebels, the imperiled remnants of human freedom, taking a stand against sadistic all-powerful global forces who are forever tightening the screws.

"Who's the More Foolish: The Fool, Or the Fool Who Follows Him?"

In *Return of the Jedi*, having finally found out who his father is, a confused and angry Luke asks Obi-Wan Kenobi: "Why didn't you tell me?" An unrepentant Kenobi responds with his famously relativistic statement about the importance of perspective to truth. He then doubles-down by admitting that the identity of

Luke's sister has also been kept from him.

This always seemed like a bad bit of escape act writing to justify the new plot development. Then again, before he found out the truth, Luke's understanding of his father's heroism in the Clone Wars helped to give him the courage to join the fight against the Empire. It made him feel significant (his father was an important man) and identified the enemy he must confront. Kenobi's stories might have been personal, but they were told for a political purpose. The most important stories are usually both.[7] Perhaps Kenobi's "half-truths" served a greater purpose?[8]

Stories don't have to be manipulations, however. Even when they are selective, which stories necessarily are, they can express deeper truths and help us to face them. The world is complicated. We create and consume stories to make sense of it, and ourselves. Ideologies are stories too. Marxist theory might suggest that one day we will be free of folklore (ideologies too), but it seems unlikely that we ever will. Nor does it seem that we want to be. As Jonathan Gottschall suggests in *The Storytelling Animal, How Stories Make Us Human*, the storytelling mind is a crucial evolutionary adaptation which allows us to experience our lives as coherent, orderly and meaningful.[9] Further, in his book *Sapiens: A Brief History of Humankind*, Yuval Noah Harari proposes that we came to dominate life on earth because we learned to cooperate flexibly in large numbers, a capacity which stems from our unique ability to create "inter-subjective realities" (money is one of these), in other words to tell stories that create bonds beyond the immediate clan.[10]

Stories have been crucial to our survival. But the wrong stories can also be our undoing, since as David Brin suggests:

[C]ivilizations turn – they veer or rise and fall – depending upon the inspirations and goals that common people share. In part, this happens through stories, heard and told, then retold, whether around a campfire or a widescreen digital display...Especially a work of art [with] the scope of influence, economic power, public exposure and relentless preachiness of the Star Wars epic.[11]

"Always in Motion Is the Future"

After all, there are two meanings of the word "myth": a false belief or idea; or a traditional story, especially one which reveals the reality of social phenomena and can include supernatural or fantastical events. One misleads, but the other can lead to truth, or at least insight.

There are hundreds of books on storytelling that claim to distill story down to a few key elements, but the essentials aren't that complicated: a person or people undergo a struggle that has an outcome. More precisely, a story is a single, unavoidable external problem that grows, escalates and complicates, forcing the protagonist(s) to make an internal change in order to solve it.[12]

Story is a particular mode of thinking, rooted not in evidential logic, but causal logic. X happens, and in reaction Y happens, and because of this, Z happens.[13] They are dynamic, a way of understanding life as a dialectic of positive and negative changes, driven by forces in conflict (like other ideologies, Marxism is a story). And crucially, stories are about an effort to restore balance. They begin when something throws life out of balance. The effort to restore balance uncovers important truths, including revealing the forces of opposition that resist this restoration.

So it is with political stories, particularly rebel stories. If we're going to reclaim the rebel story, we need to understand its common elements, as described by Orlando D'Adamo. And so: the good guys are victims of the bad guys, they blame unscrupulous politicians for letting insidious interests win, and present rebel leaders as the heroes who will recapture past righteousness. They use direct, simple, emotionally charged messages. They offer solutions, which must seem feasible, even if they aren't. They seek to recover an often mystical past, connecting people to their roots and values, and (re-)construct an identity whose reference point is a leader who defines themselves as different but historically inevitable. They also often revive founding myths (for example, America's Founding Fathers, or a society's revolutionary origins).[14]

Rebel stories have shaped history; they can change the future as well.

"You Are Unwise to Lower Your Defenses"

But these are the things that the left seems to have forgotten about telling good tales. Parts of the left, at least in Western societies, tend to prefer abstract stories where the villains are impersonal (so-called structural) forces: capitalism, the market, neoliberalism, racism, discrimination, sexism, patriarchy, forces which afflict the most vulnerable most. This is the left of rationality over emotionality, of scientific socialism, dialectical materialist Marxism, and too much difficult, dry, disempowering theory. The center-left, meanwhile, tends to focus on policy proposals as if they tell their own stories, not the big narratives as told by conservatives.[15]

It also didn't help that in response to the right's assault on welfare states in the wake of the global financial crisis, the center-left often defended the status quo. It was especially harmful that in some countries center-left parties were in power, and propped up the system, during and after the crisis, including bailing out the banks. In its accommodation to neoliberalism, the center-left had stopped telling a story that included the "rot at the top," about the malevolence of powerful elites – their corruption and irresponsibility, and tendency to conspire against the rest of us – leaving the field open for the right to tell an alternative story about supposed liberal elites.[16]

The left's stories, such that they are, are weaker than the

right's personified stories of good versus evil. There are exceptions of course. Spain's Podemos movement has told a story of the indignados (the indignant) standing up against a corrupt political class. Bernie Sanders talks of billionaires and greedy corporations, with a call that we can come together and fight back. But the latter story can still be a bit dry, resting on inequality statistics and remedial policy proposals (Medicare for All, free college tuition etc).[17]

Part of the reason is that the center-left and the left are often bad at emotion. After all, stories are linked sets of emotions and values put into dramatic action.[18] But while insurgent story forms have been used by leftist leaders, there are a number of things about such stories that can make the left nervous, including the populism, the reliance on the great leader, the identification of enemies, the divisiveness and dangers of political violence, and the cultural myth-making. Such stories seem undemocratic, indeed they can be highly undemocratic.

As Jonathan Gottschall notes, our story instinct has a dark side. It makes us vulnerable to narratives about ourselves and others that may not be true. But stories can also change the world for the better. Some commentators might assume that folklore is essentially regressive, and yet most successful stories are moral and social. They teach us how to live and bind us together through common values, often through shared outrage at villainous selfish individualism, for example against a wicked greedy figure whose hunger for power will corrupt the world.

The left, being forward-looking in wanting to build a better society, also recoils from the notion of restoring balance that is essential to many stories. It is much more likely to argue that the golden age never really existed, that many nations were founded in violence and exclusion, that there is no past to which we should want to return. The radical struggle has always been to include more people in society, not to reestablish rule by the few.[19]

And yet, as we'll argue through this book, the left happens to have in its hands a rebellion story that is political but also personal, democratic, collectivist rather than individualist, emotional and hopeful – a wildly popular saga, arguably the most successful fictional story of our time.

"That Is Why You Fail"

Yves Citton, author of *Mythocratie, Storytelling et Imaginaire de Gauche*, argues that in the wake of the global financial crisis, parts of the left lacked a rebellion story which could have united a passionate rejection of financial deregulation, denounced the outrageous profits made by traders and CEOs, and expressed disgust toward the absurdity of a system that piles stress upon stress and threat upon threat.[20]

Instead of telling its own story, the left often spends more time trying to deconstruct the right's stories (we'll explore more why this is in a moment). But as environmental campaigner and journalist George Monbiot suggests, you can't take away someone's story without giving them a new one.[21] It is not enough to challenge an old narrative, however outdated and discredited. With a new (positive, purposeful) story, everything can change.

As Yves Citton argues, we can regard populism as a sickness, or (more profitably) recognize it as manifesting the need for a politics that goes well beyond public management and the rational assessment of interests.[22] People have a desire for a new political discourse that makes room for the imaginary and for appealing stories, not as a form of denial or simplification of complex social realities, but as a recognition of its mythical quality, a reminder of the political. Reactionary myths need to be overcome by emancipatory myths. It is less important to measure how mythical stories are than to consider in which direction they push our collective development, whether they promote policies which result in a decrease or increase of our collective agency.

Yet the left reacts to this era of a "politics of the imagination" (some say post-truth) by calling for more rationality and realism. As Stephen Duncombe argues in his *Dream: Re-imagining Progressive Politics in an Age of Fantasy*, the ideological inheritors of the May '68 protest slogan of "Take your desires for reality" now counsel its reversal: take reality for your desires.[23] The left and right have effectively switched roles, the right taking on the mantle of radicalism, while progressives wave the flag of conservatism. The left needs to reclaim a politics that tells good stories and to learn again how to manufacture dissent.

"Come on, Let's Keep a Little Optimism"

This brings us into the orbit of popular culture, and explains why the left has neglected that it "owns" the most popular rebellion story of our age. What happened to the left's imagination was that it was derided and deconstructed. The left used to have its stories, its adventures, its victories and defeats involving individual and collective struggles. But scientific socialism pushed aside storytelling socialism, liberal "pragmatism" looked down on storytelling, and now, with postmodern-influenced cultural theory, stories themselves are said to be dead.

Ironically, this disdain for stories stems partly from the academic left's interest in popular culture. The left's study of culture derived from figures such as Antonio Gramsci, who argued that it must be understood as a key area of political and social struggle. In Gramsci's view, capitalists use not only brute force (police, prisons, the military) to maintain control, but also penetrate everyday culture in a variety of ways in their efforts to win popular consent, often in ways that we don't notice or recognize.[24]

But this set us off on a journey to regard stories with deep suspicion. Most obviously, the Frankfurt school reflected an avant-garde opposition to mass culture. Theodor Adorno and

14

Max Horkheimer coined the term "the culture industry" in "The Culture Industry: Enlightenment as Mass Deception" in their *Dialectic of Enlightenment* (1944).[25] The title says it all. But to expand the argument, popular culture is a factory producing standardized cultural goods that are used to pacify the masses and ensure their continued obedience to market interests, no matter how bad their economic circumstances. The culture industry cultivates false psychological needs that can only be met and satisfied by the products of capitalism.

As described in *Dialectic of Enlightenment*, the destruction of the ideals of enlightenment – which had allowed humankind to shed the shackles of myth and superstition – led to a relapse to an age of myths and superstition which set the ground for authoritarianism. For example, Adorno and Horkheimer state with regard to film that it: "...denies its audience any dimension in which they might roam freely in imagination- contained by the film's framework but unsupervised by its precise actualities."[26] Indeed, they made repeated comparisons between Fascist Germany and the American film industry, and in both highlighted the role of mass-produced culture, created and disseminated by exclusive institutions and consumed by a passive, homogenized audience.

In *Minima Moralia* (1951), Adorno further rejected the idea of cinema as art, criticizing films for being merely well-planned products of the industrial machine. It is deluded to think that individual producers actually have a say in the outcome of films (as we'll see, George Lucas would disagree), or that the culture industry ever fulfills people's genuine wishes. On the contrary, "those wholly encompassed...enjoy their own dehumanization as something human, as the joy of warmth."[27] Dehumanizing or not, it's true that people experience warmth in cultural products such as *Star Wars* – and possibly something more political as well.

"I Feel So Helpless"

Not every Marxist-influenced cultural theorist has been quite so gloomy or regarded ordinary people as quite such hopeless dupes. But we can definitely see the legacy of this view when it comes to the analysis of popular stories, including *Star Wars*.

Cultural studies informed postmodernism and its declarations about the end of big stories, although no-one seems to have told the right. Postmodernism was first described by Jean-François Lyotard in his 1979 book *The Postmodern Condition*, which proclaimed the end of the "grand narratives" considered a key feature of modernity.[28] Postmodernism has been accused of suggesting in a relativistic manner that "all stories matter," but really it has eroded intellectual confidence in *any* stories. The postmodern era is characterized by "incredulity towards metanarratives," a reluctance to think in terms of utopias and big, motivating stories of the future. Naturally, as we'll see, postmodern cultural studies tends to distrust stories such as *Star Wars*.

There have been plenty of critical responses to postmodernism, as intellectually hopeless and self-defeating, a submission to right-wing nihilism. To Ellen Meiksins Wood, the "anti-Enlightenment nonsense" associated with postmodernism distracts us that we are being asked to blame these values for the destructive effects we should be ascribing to capitalism, for example technocentrism and ecological degradation.[29] And as Andreas Malm laments, while postmodernism should have evaporated in the face of challenges such as climate change, it seems to be very much still with us, affecting the way we "write, communicate, build, plan, view, [and] imagine" far more than climate change has.[30]

Most critically, in its suspicion of stories, postmodernism induces pessimism and passivity. Despite its dangers, the philosopher Hannah Arendt believed that storytelling is vital to reopening public space and creating a more participative society.[31] It can bring hidden ideas into the mainstream. Indeed, Arendt regarded storytelling as the only real political action, because the public realm is where political decisions are taken. To participate in the construction of the common realm is to be a true hero. We don't need supermen to save us; we need to rise to the call of our own stories. That's why we tell them and consume stories, not to numb ourselves.

"I Find Your Lack of Faith Disturbing"

As Stephen Duncombe pleads:

> Progressive dreams, to have any real political impact, need to become popular dreams. This will only happen if they resonate with the dreams that people already have – like those expressed in commercial culture today...[Dreams] animate the entertainment industry and drive consumption. They can blind people to reality and provide cover for political horror. But they also inspire us to imagine that things could be radically different than they are today, and then believe we can progress toward that imaginary world.[32]

For example, science fiction has long been appreciated by its proponents as essentially political. As Walidah Imarisha and adrienne maree brown, the editors of a collection named after the black sci-fi writer Octavia E. Butler, put it: "Whenever we try to envision a world without world, without violence, without prisons, without capitalism, we are engaging in speculative fiction. All organizing is science fiction."[33] The most successful sci-fi story of our times is undoubtedly *Star Wars*. But if there are no grand narratives anymore, how come it's so popular?

You're probably not going to be persuaded that the *Star Wars* films, or at least the original trilogy (OT in saga speak), are fun, heroic, spectacular, witty and surprisingly dark if you don't want to be.[34] That doesn't really matter anyway. What's more important is recognizing that stories like *Star Wars* matter in the sense that their popularity and persistence might mean something potentially radical, that they represent hope.

Mark Fisher, the late author of *Capitalist Realism*, certainly wasn't a fan of "this depressingly mediocre franchise."[35] To Mark, capitalist realism – the belief that there is no alternative to the current economic system – means that we consume pop-culture narratives not as visions of a better world but as substitutes for it. (For the moment, we can define capitalism as a system in which our collective productive capacity is concentrated in the hands of a minority, and in which "progress" is defined by the continuous and unlimited production of commodified material wealth.[36]) Such narratives are tantalizing but harmless glimpses of a time when individuals felt that meaningful heroism was possible. In his *Ghosts of My Life*, Mark argues that *Star Wars* is a resonant example of postmodern anachronism, because its unprecedented special effects disguised the disappearance of the future as its opposite.[37]

But who says the future has disappeared? Certainly not the radicals who love this rebellion story. For example, Chris Crass, an anti-racism organizer, who traces the roots of his political values to the struggle of the Rebel Alliance against the Empire:

"[I]n true Marxist Gramscian analysis…there is a relationship between radical democratic grassroots movements disrupting unequal power and cultural shifts that advance elements of that agenda in easily digestible pedagogy, like blockbuster movies…[T]he movies only represent narrow aspects of that agenda, but [Star Wars] gives space for radical movements to gain broader support for an expansive agenda."[38]

"I Never Doubted You For a Second. Wonderful!"

Rather than being a postmodern pastiche, *Star Wars* is squarely modernist in dealing with big twentieth-century concepts such as war, revolution, empire, democracy and authoritarianism. Writing before the sequel (Disney) films, as Ajmal Khattak notes in his *A Rebel History of Star Wars* blog post, the OT and the prequels are definitely grand narratives. One is about a revolutionary struggle against all-encompassing imperial power, the other (as we'll see) is about the effect of corporations on democracy and how we descend into fascism. Both chronicle fictional galactic events based on real historical ideological and political conflicts.[39]

While the Frankfurt school saw totalitarian thought everywhere in popular culture, as we'll see in the next episode George Lucas used popular culture to locate totalitarianism specifically in the contemporary United States. At the same time, the use of a fantasy setting allows the films not to be stuck in any particular past, but to demonstrate generic models of fascism and so act as a warning for us today. Parts of the left have become so used to critiquing mass culture as reinforcing conservative or capitalist messages, we find it difficult to acknowledge when it does the opposite. Moreover, doing so might force us to take more responsibility for our own failure to tell stories that engage people.

Star Wars is also about hope and the possibilities of rebellion ("Never tell me the odds!" as Han Solo once said). Another Frankfurter, one who did recognize the importance of hope in popular stories, was Ernst Bloch. His great work was called *The Principle of Hope*, which examined the ways that popular culture, literature, political utopias, philosophy, religion and even daydreams, often dismissed as mere ideology by other Marxists, can contain emancipatory moments which project visions of a better life and challenge capitalism. Bloch believed that left thinking and politics should heed these visions to provide programs and arguments which appeal to the deep desire for a better life held by everyone.[40] We return to Bloch's ideas about utopia in episode V.

"I've Got a Good Feeling about This"

Radicals face a particular problem in telling new stories about a very different future, since by definition these can be unfamiliar compared to conservative fictions.[41] But this means all the more that we should seize on stories that audiences already know. Writing about *Rogue One*'s politics (do the Rebels represent the anti-Trump resistance?), Kate Aronoff notes that:

> Millions of people will see Star Wars this weekend...Why? Because people fucking love Star Wars. If the Left wants to write it off as politically barren so be it, but like most pop culture, its meaning will be made by the public, and by the forces best poised to take advantage of it...It's about communicating with ordinary Americans (the would-be Rebels) in terms that are as accessible as they are appealing, along with making clear that there are no Jedi powers – no high-level analysis or background in critical theory – required to help stop the creep of autocracy.[42]

We have a lot of work to do. According to a 2017 survey, the majority (53 percent) of Americans don't see *Star Wars* as political.[43] Seventeen percent think the series is political, and of that group, 41 percent are "bothered" by its political tone, but only a fifth of this group say it stops them from watching the films. Thirty percent don't know, and presumably think that pollsters should focus on more important matters.

But people's attachment to the saga could be used to tell a more political story, a rebellion story. Whatever you think about *Star Wars*, many people find it inspiring and enjoy losing (or rather, finding) themselves in its worlds and characters. They love the loyalty, bravery and camaraderie of its heroes, and love to hate the evilness, nihilism and barbarity of its villains. If capitalist realism is about the perpetual present, if it tries to convince us that nothing can ever change, perhaps the longevity of stories such as *Star Wars* can be regarded as the persistence of our belief in the possibility of a different world, whether or not we recognize such stories as political. Isn't rebellion against overwhelming, oppressive power a dream that won't die, something regenerated everyday by the ritual humiliations of capitalism, inequality and discrimination?

Rather than disguising the disappearance of the future, could it be that such stories resonate because they remind millions of us that it's ours to fight for? As Ajmal Khattak puts it:

Star Wars, probably the greatest pop-culture phenomenon in Western history, in fact belongs to the revolutionary Left. This is the Rebel History of Star Wars. It is perhaps the best-known national liberation story...To preserve the memory and meaning of the victory of the Rebel Alliance over the Empire, to "set alight the sparks of hope in the past" in that "galaxy far far away", we too must locate and attack the weak-spots of this dark machine we live under.[44]

A New Hope had audiences cheering the defeat of an imperial force by a ragbag band of guerrillas just a couple of years after the disastrously drawn-out end of the Vietnam War. It's the most politically radical popular film of the past 50 years. It was, and is, huge. Rather than retreating into postmodern passivity, we need to return to hope and human agency to tell tales of resistance and rebellion, including by drawing on popular culture. Sure, let's critique and criticize *Star Wars*, but when it comes to its popularity, lefty commentators might want to reconsider their tendency to snatch defeat from the Jaw(a)s of victory.

"Your Feelings Betray You"

I know, because I made the same mistake. Around the time that the prequels were being released, if I thought about the saga at all it was to buy into the tragic version of the George Lucas story, in which a talented young experimental filmmaker is corrupted by unprecedented success. I secretly wanted his new films to fail.

I recognize now that this was really about love. I loved *A New Hope*, which was the first film I remember seeing at the cinema (it wasn't called *A New Hope* in 1977 of course). I grew up with the OT, played with the toys (little did we realize they were early political education in plastic) and acted out its famous scenes on the school playground. We all did. *Star Wars* was our story.

When the prequels rolled out, I wasn't one of the millions whose voices cried out in terror that "George Lucas ruined my childhood!" I recognized that *Star Wars* had (to) become a story for a new generation. But somehow, I felt vindicated by the critical reaction they received. Simon Pegg captured how we felt in an episode of the British cult TV comedy *Spaced*: "You weren't there at the beginning! You don't know how good it was, how important! This is it for you, this jumped-up display of a toy advert. People like you make me sick, what's wrong with you?" Cut to reveal that he's ranting at a prequel-loving child.

The acquisition of Lucasfilm by Disney only served to confirm my Gen-X prejudices. Of course Lucas sold out to a theme park, to a corporate empire. But in early 1978, already fed up with simple-minded commentary, Denis Wood, a geographer by profession, wrote one of the first serious pieces about this growing phenomenon:

Whatever the differences separating commentators on Star Wars...they are united on one point: both insist on the movie's simplistic moral vision and naive characterizations. Whether it is because of the film's unusually gripping story and breathtakingly rapid pace, or because it fails to display those stigmata so appealing to the pseudo-intellectuals dominant in international film criticism – or both – is difficult to say, but the fact is that neither camp has been able to get its blast shields up long enough to see, much less understand the movie.[45]

What I remember is that, as kids, we absolutely got it. *Star Wars* was about fighting for your friends and freedom. It was fun, and yes, it seemed *important* somehow to fight space fascists. Wood called a later analysis on *A New Hope* "growing up among the stars." He meant Luke's maturation in the story, but it went for us as well.

Hope was important to hang onto in the 1980s, as the new right revolution overturned the republic (we'll talk about that in a later episode). And looking back, I realize now that stories such as *Star Wars* can help us hang onto hope. Not a naive hope, but the most important hope of all, that heroism and humane values, the forces within us, can combine to fight oppression and bring freedom and justice to our world. Because if we don't believe that, what is (the) left?[46]

Episode II

"Rebellions Are Built on Hope"

"You Must Unlearn What You Have Learned"

From George Lucas's notes in late 1973, which chart his evolving ideas for *The Star Wars* [sic]:

> Theme: Aquilae is a small independent country like North Vietnam threatened by a neighbor or provincial rebellion, instigated by gangsters aided by empire...The empire is like America ten years from now, after gangsters assassinated the Emperor and were elevated to power in a rigged election...We are at a turning point: fascism or revolution.[1]

Star Wars is a fable rooted in the 1960s American new left, a warning about creeping authoritarianism, but also a beacon of new hope to rebels everywhere.

It's strange then, as Will Brooker notes in his BFI Film Classics appraisal, that cinema scholarship seems to be embarrassed by *Star Wars*, to the extent that it mainly discusses the film in relation to its audiences, special effects, merchandising and impact on the studio system, rather than its themes, story and characters.[2] This goes back to some of the first reviews, for example Pauline Kael on *A New Hope*:

> [I]t's a film that's totally uninterested in anything that doesn't connect with the mass audience...It's enjoyable on its own terms, but it's exhausting, too: like taking a pack of kids to the circus...The excitement of those who call it the film of the year goes way past nostalgia to the feeling that now is the time to return to childhood.[3]

It's true that *Star Wars* was meant for kids, but this is partly what makes it subversive. It was meant to introduce a new generation to folklore, which George Lucas felt they were missing.

The classic myth is the tale of someone, typically a young person, taking their first steps into a larger world and learning to give themselves to something bigger.[4] Drawing on story architypes, *Star Wars* is a modern fairy tale. Moreover, as we'll see, it was steeped in a worldview that the world has been corrupted and needs to be challenged through radical action led by a new generation.

Denis Wood made an important observation about this accusation of childishness. In the context of a bourgeois society, both popular stories and folktales "have been relegated to the nursery."[5] In the nineteenth century, storytelling became mainly an entertainment of the poor. The middle classes professed to prefer "rational thinking" and modern mass media to community-based narrative oral entertainment involving archetypal characters. Calling something "childish" is a way for the bourgeois to distance themselves from stories, from the masses and crucially, as we'll note, from taking action to change society.

"I Feel the Good in You, the Conflict"

Imagine an alternative universe in which *A New Hope* wasn't a success. There having been no sequels, it's periodically re-discovered as a radical kids movie, a strange little '70s hippie experiment that never found an audience. That's not how it turned out, of course. More than just a hit movie, *Star Wars* became "a celebration, a social affair, a collective dream."[6]

So was born the cliché of a young experimental filmmaker who went to the dark side, corrupted by an empire of plastic. Lucas has acknowledged that *Star Wars* became so successful that it took over his life. Speaking before the prequels, Francis Ford Coppola lamented of his friend and former business partner that:

"The great success of Star Wars didn't lead to the independence and personal filmmaking. George never made another film after that...And instead we have a kind of enormous industrial marketing complex."[7]

Star Wars has certainly been used to shovel a lot of crap, but the merchandise is a function of its massive popularity. Young and old want to spend time in its universe. The toys allow kids to play out their own stories of rebellion on rainy days and during long hot summers. Meanwhile, adult fans avidly consume different corners of the saga. Some "just" find comedy, camaraderie and inspiration in it. But geeks' engagement can also be a form of creative rebellion.[8] As Jase Short has noted, what defines a geek is their hostility to passive consumption: "For one, there are few if any committed fans who aren't aware of the various forms of capitalist intellectual property constraints that dominate the cultural products in question."[9] Nonetheless, many do re-engineer these products, for example the huge number of fan edits of the much-maligned prequels that can be found online. The toys were the old means of creating your own *Star Wars* story. Now you can effectively reshoot the saga.[10]

In a widely-discussed piece called *The Complex and Terrifying Reality of Star Wars Fandom*, Andrey Summers captures it like this:

> To be a Star Wars fan, one must possess the ability to see a million different failures and downfalls, and then somehow assemble them into a greater picture of perfection. Every true Star Wars fan is a Luke Skywalker, looking at his twisted, evil father, and somehow seeing good...[The fans] hate everything about Star Wars. But the idea of Star Wars...the idea we love.[11]

We'll return to fandom, and particularly its dark side, later on, but for the moment let's ask: what is this idea that has taken a hold of so many people?

"No, I Am Your Father"

Lucas's debut feature, the experimental *THX-1138* (1971), depicted a soulless future society where brutal robotic police, videogames and drugs subdue the population. An underdog fights back against the oppressive system, the machine. According to its director, the message was: "Modern society is a rotten thing. If you're smart you'll start an alternative civilization above ground, out of the sewer you find yourself in."[12]

THX tanked. Audiences didn't want to be reminded of their alienation on a night out. Studio interference in this and his next film, *American Graffiti*, reinforced Lucas's distaste for authority and convinced him that he needed absolute control over his work. He wanted to retain the licensing (merchandising) rights to *Star Wars* because he thought that the studio wouldn't promote it, so toys and T-shirts would have to do the job instead.

With its enormous success, Lucas became the only filmmaker who has ever managed to make big budget movies with his own money, as well as establishing numerous successful subsidiaries such as special effects house Industrial Light & Magic. It might be too much to claim, as Lucas once did, that through his companies, "The workers have the means of production."[13] But he certainly found a way to avoid the adults telling him what to do.

This attitude runs through the movies made under Lucas, the biggest independent films of all time. As he acknowledged, "I've always had a basic dislike of authority figures, a fear and resentment of grown-ups," manifested most obviously in the brooding malevolence of Darth Vader ("dark father," though Lucas denies this was intentional).[14]

Lucas's feelings about authority had many influences, for example *MAD* magazine:

Parents, school, sex, politics, religion, big business, advertising and popular culture, using humor to show the emperor had no clothes. This helped me recognize that just because something is presented to you as the way it is, doesn't mean that's really the way it really is. I realized that if I wanted to see a change in the status quo, I couldn't rely on the world to do it for me.[15]

As Camille Paglia notes, Lucas's youthful liberalism (versus his father's rock-ribbed conservatism) was typical of bohemian 1960s San Francisco, a hotbed of radical politics and psychedelia.[16] (Paglia, by the way, regards Lucas as the greatest artist of our time.) Despite being aimed at children, *Star Wars* had a broad appeal from the beginning. But as noticed by some early commentators on the right, it was propelled by a specific generational perspective. Richard Grenier, writing in *Commentary* magazine just after *The Empire Strikes Back*, derided the series as a "hodgepodge of 'anti-materialist' pieties salvaged from the detritus of the counterculture": "It is ironic, now that so many of the radical and revolutionary leaders of the 60s and early 70s have scampered back into the political mainstream, that their attitudes are now being voiced by a True Child, in what is after all the appropriate medium of a children's story."[17]

Generationally, *Star Wars* looks in two different directions. It occupied the imaginations of the kids (like me) who would become the Gen Xers, but it was born of the rebellion by the baby boomers against their parents. As Mark Fisher notes in *Capitalist Realism*, the protest impulse of the 1960s posited a malevolent Father who cruelly and arbitrarily denies the "right" to enjoyment and hoards resources.[18] Although Mark didn't approve of the series, the most famous revelation in cinema history dramatizes his point. When at the end of *The Empire Strikes Back*, Darth Vader reveals himself as Luke's father, the personal and the political, the man and the machine, fuse into one. Fascism's mean Father figure is...your actual father.

"It's a Trap!"

To a number of critics at the time and ever since, rather than being political, *A New Hope* only provided a fantastical distraction from politics. The American public had recently learned that their government was a cancerous conspiracy (Watergate) and that, against the country's self-image, they were hated imperialists (the Vietnam War). Despite President Gerald Ford pardoning the corrupt Richard Nixon and declaring that "Our long national nightmare is over," many Americans thought they recognized the foul stench of a rotting republic all around them.

Other critics acknowledge *Star Wars'* anti-authority theme but argue that it promotes a conservative agenda. For example, Michael Ryan and Douglas Kellner, in their *Camera Politica: Politics and Ideology in Contemporary Hollywood Film*, suggest that *Star Wars* was one of a slew of stories which struck back against socially-critical New Hollywood movies of the time such as *Easy Rider, Bonnie and Clyde* and *Medium Cool*.[19] *A New Hope* helped to popularize the Reagan revolution by vilifying the state and promoting conservative individualism.[20] To this view, *Star Wars* may have echoed 1960s' Californian counter-culturalism but assimilated these values into the Reagan-Thatcher conservativism of the 1980s.[21]

To commentators such as Tom Engelhardt, *Star Wars* was an attempt to mend America's broken myth from its experience in Vietnam by going back to "morally safe" wars in which the United States played a winning role, hence the Nazi-styled Empire, and even to America's Revolutionary War and Western frontier folklore. In perhaps the ultimate act of cultural appropriation of the war in South East Asia, *Star Wars* allowed America to think of itself once again as a republic of rebel heroes.[22]

Mumia Abu-Jamal offers a related but more contingent take:

In the grisly aftermath of a war that tore millions from the face of Asia...the imperial shock trooper, the imperial, metallic death's hand, was father to the rebel. They were, in fact, more than related. In truth, they were one. That is the meaning of Star Wars: we were rebels; we are Empire. And like all rebellious children, we were but going through a phase...Once grown, we put on our imperial uniform, and bowed to the Empire. "It is your destiny." Right? Unless –[23]

"It Is Our Destiny!"

Lucas acknowledges that he wrote *Star Wars* because society was in need of myths, but not as a distraction from what was going on. He explained that, "I love history, so while the psychological basis of Star Wars is mythological, the political and social bases are historical."[24] *Star Wars* is contemporary folklore about the rise and defeat of fascism (and rise again, as the latest films demonstrate).

To start with, the Second World War, which was folklore to the young people of the 1970s, resonates throughout the series. The Rebellion's lowest points echo Europe's darkest hours under the spreading shadow of fascism, the Alliance overmatched against the expansionary, technologically-superior Empire. It's also reflected in the chunky armor-plated space ships, the turbolaser turrets and dogfights.[25]

Within the first half an hour of *A New Hope*, Darth Vader strangles/suffocates two people, one of them during a staff meeting. Stormtroopers incinerate Luke's aunt and uncle and massacre the underclass Jawas. The dead-eyed Grand Moff Tarkin orders the torture of Princess Leia, and when she resists, the annihilation of billions of people on the planet Alderaan in a demonstration of mechanized genocide.[26] The Imperials refer repeatedly to destiny, inevitability and fate, and believe that their 1000-year space Reich is supported by a mystical historical force. Ambiguous about authoritarianism, this children's movie is not.

The wretched hive of scum and villainy that is Mos Eisley also has the flavor of an occupied *Casablanca*. Like that movie, another great popular entertainment made for propaganda purposes (to get the United States to join the fight against fascism), *Star Wars* is about the importance of standing up. At first (and rather contrary to the deleted scene with Biggs), Luke whines that: "It's not like I like the Empire, I hate it, but there's nothing I can do about it right now." Later, Han (a space pirate Humphrey Bogart) makes his "neutrality" clear: "Look, I ain't in this for your revolution...I'm in it for the money." Thankfully, seeing what his friends are up against, he too finally joins the fight.

"Stay on Target"

Star Wars' other touchstone was Vietnam. Like many young Americans, George Lucas was desperate to avoid the tractor beam of the draft to serve in South East Asia. While at the University of Southern California studying film, he tried to join the Air Force in the hope of becoming an officer in the photography unit. He was rejected because of the numerous speeding tickets from his days zooming around his home town of Modesto (these experiences later informed *American Graffiti*).[27]

Another result of the failure of *THX-1138* was Lucas's next planned project, *Apocalypse Now*, at the time conceived as a low-budget darkly satirical documentary-style film about the Vietnam War in the style of *Dr Strangelove*. Instead:

A lot of my interest in Apocalypse Now carried over into Star Wars...I figured that I couldn't make that film because it was about the Vietnam War, so I would essentially deal with some of the same interesting concepts that I was going to use and convert them into space fantasy, so you'd have essentially a large technological empire going after a small group of freedom fighters or human beings.[28]

Conservative commentators tend to grasp what Lucas was up to far more readily than those on the left. For example, Arthur Chrenkoff, writing in the Australian *Spectator*, warns conservatives that *Star Wars* has always been a radical left fantasy:

"[T]he...evil Empire is [the] United States, and the heroes, the good guys that we, the viewers, are meant to root for, are the communist guerrillas...[T]he American Empire was a quasi-fascistic, semi-dictatorial, highly aggressive and militaristic polity in the grip of "the military-industrial complex" and "the power elites", suppressing dissent and subjugating minorities at home, while continuously invading poor Third World countries to crush their national aspirations in the interests of the American corporations and the American war machine."[29]

Well, indeed. Or as the sculptor John Powers puts it on his *Star Wars Modern* blog: "Thanks to George Lucas's ploy, an entire generation of American boys would identify with the underdogs of asymmetrical warfare. Within the belly of an aggressive nuclear super power, we were innocently rooting against our own team. We were all fighting for the Rebellion."[30]

"Something Inside Me Has Always Been There, but Now It's Awake"

Lucas's political perspective came from the 1960s new left, which rejected the anti-democratic nature of "old left" bureaucratic Marxist-Communist parties as well as contemporary capitalism and conventional center-left politics. The new left was anti-imperialist and emphasized grassroots democracy.

In the US, the movement was most associated with anti-war

college-campus protests, including Students for a Democratic Society (SDS), and the Free Speech Movement. The latter started during the 1964-1965 academic year on the campus of the University of California at Berkeley. In response to ridiculous suggestions that the movement was being directed by outside (communist) forces, Jack Weinberg captured its generational stance when he famously declared that: "We have a saying in the movement that you can't trust anyone over 30."

Student-led activism came to a head in 1968. In the US, the wave that began with the civil rights movement was reaching its height (the civil rights movement preceded the anti-war movement but became more radical in the second half of the decade). Social movements were on the rise from West Germany and Japan, Mexico and Italy, to Canada and Denmark, Yugoslavia and the UK. The beach of alternative possible worlds was being glimpsed beneath the paving stones of a dull post-war conservatism.[31] The French government was nearly toppled by what was then the largest general strike in world history, while the German student movement temporarily shut down Bonn. Universities were occupied. The rebellion even spread to high schools.

As Richard Vinen notes, '68 had several components: a generational rebellion of the young against the old (a distinct youth identity being a relatively new phenomenon), a political rebellion against militarism, capitalist consumerism and the power of the United States, and a cultural rebellion that revolved around lifestyle and rock music.[32] There was also a growing international awareness, most notably of experiences of Western imperialism. Sometimes these rebellions interacted. They also challenged structures on the left, for example traditional trade unions, or patriarchy through feminism and gay liberation – revolutions within the revolution.[33]

In reality, there was a "long '68" with a lasting influence, some of it still ongoing.[34]

The protests continued. Hundreds of thousands of young Americans took to the streets in marches during 1969 and 1970. Some felt the country came close to civil war. SDS founder Tom Hayden claimed that the anti-war movement, "...reached a scale which threatened the foundations of the American social order, making it an inspirational model for future social movements and a nightmare which elites ever since have hoped to wipe from memory."[35]

The new left was also a set of demands for a better republic: for greater rights and democracy, the recognition of marginalized and disadvantaged groups, and social, economic and environmental justice. The writer Kirkpatrick Sale called them the "awakened generation."[36] To Douglas Murphy, what happened to the radical '60s and '70s as a whole was possibly the last chance the West had of creating a decent and environmentally sustainable society. These radical movements believed that other futures and new ways of living were possible, even inevitable.[37]

"Rebel Scum"

Perhaps the most famous declaration of new left views was the *Port Huron Statement*, also known as the *Agenda for a Generation*, a 25,700-word manifesto drafted by SDS members in June 1962. This articulated the fundamental problems of American society. It was a non-ideological call for participatory democracy (it brought the term into common parlance), as a means and an end, to be achieved through nonviolent civil disobedience.

The statement also observed the apathy and powerlessness of ordinary people, and their separation from power and decision-making. Way before postmodern analysis, it noted that, "The decline of utopia and hope is in fact one of the defining features of social life today...To be idealistic is to be considered apocalyptic, deluded." And as would be echoed in Lucas's allusion of the Empire to contemporary America, Port Huron argued that "the American political system is not the democratic model of which its glorifiers speak. In actuality it frustrates democracy by confusing the individual citizen, paralyzing policy discussion, and consolidating the irresponsible power of military and business interests." Nevertheless, the final introductory words of statement declared that: "If we appear to seek the unattainable...we do so to avoid the unimaginable."

George Lucas wasn't a new left leader, but he was immersed in its political culture. He attended USC Film School in the early 1960s and re-enrolled as a graduate student from 1967-1968. He claimed of his time at university, "I was angry at the time, getting involved in all the causes."[38]

Like many young people, Lucas was a first-hand witness to an American civil war. *Star Wars* would transport this into space. *A New Hope* can then be read as somewhat autobiographical. As Dave Schilling put it: "Luke Skywalker wasn't that far removed from the Berkeley freshman getting a crash course in What's Really Going On from his radical professors."[39]

Relatedly, John Powers interprets *Star Wars* as a counter to the Cold War anti-communism of politicians like Richard Nixon, who used the phantom menace of "leftist infiltration" to justify the domestic control of radical political groups. Lucas imagined a battle against a total control police state that had turned inward against its own citizens. In part because of this backlash, the new left faltered and fractured. Some splinters became violent, perhaps the inspiration of *Star Wars'* warnings about being led by hatred and anger. To Powers, the hope in *Star Wars* calls out to the (only temporarily) lost dreams of the new left:

With Star Wars, Lucas gave the rebels he associated himself with a single concrete victory over an easily identifiable villain (Space Nazis). These concrete villains and victories echoed the far-less concrete constellation of victories that had left youthful liberals discouraged. Perhaps Lucas's genius was delivering a triumphant reward [that] no real-world victory had actually delivered, at a time when alienation and cynicism passed for common sense.[40]

Powers doesn't say it, but *Star Wars*, released in the same year that punk exploded, shared some of the same militant rage against the machine.[41] It just did it in a family-friendly, accessible form. And in the end of course, its lesson is that the Force is superior to the machine.

"If You Only Knew the Power of the Dark Side"

The *Star Wars* prequels have been derided by many critics and fans, though they've undergone a re-evaluation of late. But their most important contribution is to dramatize, however shakily, that the Empire didn't arise outside of the Republic but grew within it. As Lucas explains:

> When I first started making [*A New Hope*], it was during the Vietnam War, and it was during a period when Nixon was going for a third term – or trying to get the Constitution changed to go for a third term – and it got me to thinking about how democracies turn into dictatorships. Not how they're taken over where there's a coup or anything like that, but how the democracy turns itself over to a tyrant.[42]

The political story of the prequels is how the big business Sith alliance manufactures a crisis and seizes on the desire of a frustrated public for strong leadership to master the chaos (how corporate capitalism erodes democracy is discussed more in the next episode). Chancellor Palpatine is granted emergency powers that open the door to militarization, repression including the liquidation of the Jedi, and the establishment of dictatorship.[43] Lucas further reflects that:

> You sort of see these recurring themes where a democracy

turns itself into a dictatorship, and it always seems to happen kind of in the same way...A democratic body, a senate, not being able to function properly because everybody's squabbling, there's corruption...The Empire is like America ten years from now, after Nixonian gangsters assassinated the Emperor and were elevated to power in a rigged election...[44]

When Lucas first started writing, it was the age of concerns about the "imperial presidency" – the concentration of power in the chief executive under the all-purpose invocation of "national security," a result of the permanent emergency of the Cold War, the Korean and Vietnam Wars and nuclear rivalry with the Soviet Union. The imperial presidency extended from foreign into domestic affairs. Historian Arthur Schlesinger Jr.'s classic study *The Imperial Presidency* (1973) identified its executive secrecy, withholding of information from Congress, intimidation of the press and use of the White House for espionage and the sabotage of political opponents.

As Anne Lancashire notes, the *Star Wars* prequels echo this in emphasizing the corrupting influence of militarism on democracy, a major new left theme. War in *Attack of the Clones* is depicted as a tool supported by profit-seeking big business, the means by which manipulative leaders achieve power by exploiting fear and greed.[45]

Despite the backstory being sketched out many years before, the prequels hit a particular political resonance on their release in the late 1990s/early 2000s, mirroring the erosion of personal liberties and government accountability under the War on Terror. Anakin Skywalker echoes President George W. Bush in stating, "If you're not with me, you're my enemy." (Obi-Wan responds that "Only a Sith deals in absolutes.") Lucas was explicit in interviews, comparing Bush to Nixon and the invasion of Iraq to Vietnam. When one interviewer compared Vice President Dick Cheney to Darth Vader, Lucas corrected her: "George Bush is

Darth Vader. Cheney is the Emperor."[46]

Despite some critical reviews then, the prequel trilogy not only introduced the saga to a new generation but also to timely political themes: war, terror, corruption, the hollowing out of democracy by fascism, fearful populaces and the seductions of "security"...themes which, as we'll see, these generations are more than aware of.

"So You're with the Resistance?"

J. J. Abrams, the director of *The Force Awakens*, said the concept for the First Order (the new Empire) "came out of conversations about what would have happened if the Nazis all went to Argentina but then started working together again."

The allusions aren't subtle. The white-power rally on Starkiller Base is decorated with banners evoking real fascist regimes. One new character, the fleeing stormtrooper Finn, played by the black British actor John Boyega, reveals that he was raised by the Empire as a slave and has no name. The implicit racism of the OT's coldly technocratic Empire becomes explicit in the First Order's rant-fueled fanaticism.

But at least to begin with, the Disney era films didn't seem to have the same political preoccupations as their predecessors. If the prequels suffered from too much exposition, the retro *Force Awakens* rushed to get back into the action without sufficiently establishing the context.[47] Who exactly are the First Order and how are they different from the Empire? What exactly is the relationship between the Resistance and the New Republic? Perhaps the pull of the empire versus rebels' story template was just too strong to resist.[48]

However, the second sequel, *The Last Jedi*, stepped more decisively into politics, most obviously in the mission undertaken by Finn and Rose to the planet Canto Bight, where the galaxy's one percenters (including war profiteers) gorge themselves at an intergalactic casino. Our rebels trash the place by releasing a stampede of space horses (fathiers), after Rose, who grew up in a poor mining colony, provides some impromptu class education to Finn on how it feels to live under a regime of exploitation (she shouldn't really need to, given Finn's background).

Intentionally or otherwise, *The Last Jedi* became a focus in the ongoing culture wars, with complaints about its characters (too many powerful women!), casting (racial diversity!), incongruous humor (actually, there are some valid criticisms here) and plotting (again not completely unfair, but the saga has always made illogical story turns). *The Force Awakens* had stirred the right with its casting, but its fan-service feel quelled some of the passions. No longer.

The Kylo Rens of the internet have taken against the series, urging moviegoers to #DumpStarWars because of its social justice warriorship and demanding that its owners Make Star Wars Great Again (of course, it's possible to dislike *The Last Jedi* without being drawn to the dark side). At the time of writing, it remains to be seen whether *The Rise of Skywalker* will choose a side in this particular civil war, between the self-declared Fandom Menace and the much larger group of fans who believe that *Star Wars* is for everybody and so #SWRepMatters.

"Aren't You a Little Short for a Stormtrooper?"

Despite the OT's lack of diversity, *Star Wars* has always avoided what we'd now regard as toxic masculinity in its heroes, reflecting George Lucas's '60s San Franciscoism. Even Han learns that it's okay to embrace an Ewok. Rather, any will-to-power fantasies have always been reserved for the saga's villains.

Now, when conservatives call for a return to "escapism," it's because they want to re-establish ownership over a culture changing around them. When they bemoan "politics" being "forced" into their favorite saga it's because they've previously not seen anything political in the dominance of white, cisgendered, heterosexual men in heroic leading roles.[49]

Then again, there's nothing new in the right's antipathy to "Hollywood." Conservatives have regularly tried to establish and exploit a divide between "regular folks" and "liberal elites," from the Red Scares of McCarthyism to Ronald Reagan's rhetorical religiosity against his godless former employers. Because of its apparently uncontroversial simplicity, and because so many people love it, *Star Wars* had largely avoided attack, until now.

Unfortunately for the right, anti-elitism runs through *The Last Jedi* in particular, echoing the critiques of the previous films made by the science fiction writer David Brin and others.[50] A grizzled Luke Skywalker (hiding away like the hermits Ben Kenobi of *A New Hope* and Yoda of *The Empire Strikes Back*) denounces his old Order: "[I]t's time for the Jedi to end...the legacy of the Jedi is failure, hypocrisy, hubris." As Toby Moses notes, the film subverts the series and hero stories generally by presenting a rebellion in which:

[A]nybody can be a hero, so there's no excuse not to get involved in the fight...If the original trilogy was about waiting for a hero to rescue the world from a tyrannical, authoritarian regime, and the prequels were an (albeit ham fisted) attempt to examine how democracy can easily mutate in to dictatorship...[Rian] Johnson's entry has rooted the future of the series in a populist framework of how to defeat tyranny through community.[51]

Perhaps it was this that really provoked such ire among some fans and conservative commentators. *The Last Jedi* says we need to let yesterday die, kill it if we have to, in its challenges to saga lore and in the battle between the past and the future represented by its main protagonists Kylo Ren (angry heir to the Skywalker dynasty) and Rey (a "nobody" – or is she?). The hope that survives rests not in the individual hero's journey, but in the collective – in the depleted but determined remnants of the Resistance, now the Rebellion. The right looks to strong leaders ("I AM the senate!" as Palpatine declares). In the rebellion, we look to each other.

"Only Now, at the End, Do You Understand"

Going further, the first *Star Wars* spin-off movie *Rogue One* presents the Rebellion from the perspective of its regular foot soldiers, a way more diverse bunch than in the OT. Just after Trump's election, its writer Chris Weitz (with Tony Gilroy) tweeted that, "Please note that the Empire is a white supremacist (human) organization." (It's true: Palpatine's putsch imposes a white male human government on the galaxy.) *Rogue One* contributor Gary Whitta added: "Opposed by a multi-cultural group led by brave women."[52]

The second spin-off, *Solo*, seemed to represent a return to the kind of old-school "non-political" *Star Wars* conservatives claim they crave. Even so, there's a prominent anti-exploitation theme running through the movie. It starts on the Dickensian-feeling Corellia, Han Solo's ship-building home planet under the control of the Empire, where child orphan "scrumrats" are indentured to criminal gangs (we also learn that Han's father was laid off from one of the planet's factories). Later it reaches out to a planet being colonized by Imperial forces. As a new recruit, the young Han questions the Empire's attempted occupation, to no avail. Finally, we venture out to the wilder wastelands dominated by vicious crime syndicates, where luxury space yachts glide above poverty-stricken communities scarred by resource extraction.

In all of these locations, as implied but never really explored in the previous films, both *Rogue One* and especially *Solo* depict the corruption and coercion which runs rampant under the "peace and security" of the Empire. Indeed, the suggestion is that there's no real difference between criminal gangs and the Empire in their oppression and exploitation of anything and anyone.

In *Solo*, we also meet what we think at first are just another band of space pirates but who turn out to be fighters trying to stop the rampant exploitation. Their leader, Enfys Nest, explains that Crimson Dawn is not just a criminal organization but an ally of the Empire. She and her band of pirates are starting a rebellion...

Despite its male lead, alt-right "fans" were mightily pleased with themselves in tagging the film "Soylo," a reference to soyboys, supposedly weak males with low testosterone who consume vegan products and who willingly "submit" to the demands of "female supremacists."

"This is not my *Star Wars*!" cry conservatives. They're right, but it never was. The saga, despite its faults, has always been an anti-fascist fable. With its new left roots, *Star Wars* has also long been part of the culture wars, though few noticed it to begin with. But it's symptomatic of today's right that it throws a tantrum about anything it thinks it owns. They literally don't like others playing with their toys. Having ventured into the dark cave, only now do some conservatives recognize their own face beneath Vader's cracked mask and realize that they're not the heroes of the story but its villains.

"Do, or Do Not Do. There Is No Try"

Five years after *A New Hope* and 2 years after the darker *The Empire Strikes Back*, audiences were treated to another visionary depiction of the future in *Blade Runner*. Harrison Ford's involvement meant that many filmgoers were expecting another rollicking sci-fi adventure. What they got, the relatively few who saw it at the time, was a dour, dank neo-noir. But Pauline Kael still wasn't happy: "[Blade Runner] treats this grimy, retrograde future as a given – a foregone conclusion, which we're not meant to question...The sci-fi movies of the past were often utopian or cautionary; this film seems indifferent, blasé...satisfied in a slightly vengeful way."[53]

As Kael noted, *Blade Runner*'s world has gone to shit, but nobody tries to change it, yet alone rebel against its towering mega-corporations (the replicant "skin jobs" do revolt, but out of a desperate desire to extend their lifespans).

Historian Jill Lepore has identified a radical pessimism in contemporary dystopian fiction. Whereas it used to be a "fiction of resistance," it has now become a "fiction of submission," of helplessness and hopelessness.[54] In contrast, *Star Wars*, which is deeply unfashionable in cultural theory compared to *Blade Runner*, doesn't just depict a dystopian future but focuses on fighting it. It says that another galaxy is possible.

This agency is what Cass Sunstein, a leading constitutional scholar, thinks *Star Wars* is all about, our ability to make the right decision when it really matters. Sunstein, who among other things pioneered the study of "choice architecture," emphasizes that the main characters in *Star Wars* are resolutely active: "Star Wars also makes a bold claim about freedom of choice. Whenever people find themselves in trouble, or at some kind of crossroads, the series proclaims: *You are free to choose…*the foundation of its rousing tribute to human freedom."[55]

The real contrast between *Star Wars* and the socially-critical New Hollywood movies of the late 1960s and 1970s is then that in *Star Wars* resistance is not futile; there's always a chance that the system can be beaten.

Similarly, to Denis Wood, the momentum of *A New Hope*, which many critics dismissed as mere childish hyperactivity, is core to its meaning: "To orient yourself in this crazy living serendipitous universe you turn to Luke – and thereby realize there is nothing, in this or any other universe, preventing you from being human each and every moment of your life."[56] This is why *Star Wars* is dismissed as childish: it allows us to distance ourselves from taking action, from "real living, consulting your feelings instead of your attitudes, your being instead of your position, your sense of humanity instead of your career line."

Moreover, throughout the series, it's often the female characters who are the most independently-minded, from Princess Leia resisting the Empire within the Senate while secretly helping to lead the Rebellion, and Padmé Amidala's story of a young woman's difficult political awakening as the true nature of the phantom menace reveals itself, to self-reliant scavenger Rey's journey to resistance in the sequel trilogy, and Jyn Erso's revolutionary leadership in *Rogue One*.[57] From *A New Hope* to *The Rise of Skywalker*, political authority and military leadership in the Rebellion/Resistance is typically vested in female characters.[58]

Perhaps this agency is what really lies at the heart of Frankfurt-style dislike of *Star Wars*. The series says that, despite everything, we can rip out our constraining bolts and challenge the system. An unjust universe has no place for academic armchair pessimism, since as George Lucas argued:

If you can't do anything about the Empire, the Empire will eventually crush you ...To not make a decision is a decision... What usually happens is a small minority stands up against it, and the major portion are a lot of indifferent people who aren't doing anything one way or the other. By not accepting the responsibility, those people eventually have to confront the issue in a more painful way – which is essentially what happened in the United States with the Vietnam War.[59]

In the next episode we go to the dark side to uncover empire's sinister plans. For the moment, perhaps we can see in the *Star Wars* saga what Howard Zinn reminds us of in *A Power Governments Cannot Suppress*:

To be hopeful in bad times is not just foolishly romantic. It is based on the fact that human history is a history not only of

cruelty, but also of compassion, sacrifice, courage, kindness...
And if we do act, in however small a way, we don't have to
wait for some grand utopian future. The future is an infinite
succession of presents, and to live now as we think human
beings should live, in defiance of all that is bad around us, is
itself a marvelous victory.[60]

Episode III

"Nothing Will Stand in Our Way"

"Once You Start Down the Dark Path, Forever Will It Dominate Your Destiny"

Once upon a time, the right claimed the light side of the Force for themselves. Echoing some critics on the academic left, in this reading *A New Hope* heralded a cultural shift that preceded the election of Margaret Thatcher in 1979 and Ronald Reagan a year later. Here was a morality tale of individuals standing up against a suffocating statist bureaucracy, and at its worst, a Stalinist war machine.[1] *Star Wars* reasserted traditional values in an America that was becoming increasingly secular and relativistic. And Cold War warrior Reagan liked to employ simple *Star Wars*-like analogies, including describing the Soviet Union as an evil empire.[2]

But over time, conservatives have increasingly come to embrace the Empire. Since *Star Wars* can be used as a mirror to our own times and politics, we should listen to them when they tell us who they really are.

This turn really started to happen around the time of the prequels as the anti-authoritarian politics of Lucas's story became unavoidable and the Empire apologists revealed themselves (not that they had really been that much in hiding). In 2002 for example, as *Attack of the Clones* hit theaters, Jonathan Last made "The Case for the Empire" in the conservative *Weekly Standard*. Apparently, "The deep lesson of 'Star Wars' is that the Empire is good." Sure, Palpatine is a dictator, but a "relatively benign one." Last then added: "...like Pinochet."[3]

This wasn't the first time the right has expressed support for General Augusto Pinochet's 1973 military coup in Chile against a democratically-elected government, and with it the oppression, torture and murder of political opponents. Many conservatives have praised the regime, at the time and subsequently, for "restoring order." What they're really defending is the neoliberal economic experiment inflicted on the country's citizens, which produced widespread poverty and suffering.

Last conveniently ignores how the Empire's promise of order against the "aimless violent anarchists" of the Rebel Alliance is a lie. The regime is actually criminal, corrupt and chokingly bureaucratic, as fascist states are in real life. Nonetheless, *Weekly Standard* editor William Kristol returned to the argument for *The Force Awakens*: "Needless to say, I was rooting for the Empire from the first moment. It was a benevolent liberal empire, after all."[4]

Even worse, Sonny Bunch breezily suggested in *The Washington Post* in 2015 that the destruction of Alderaan was completely justified: "Alderaan was less likely a peaceful planet than a financial and intellectual hub of the rebellion...Granted, you have to use force once for the threat to be useful, but it's easy to see the appeal of such a tactic, which is designed to save lives in the long run."[5]

The *National Review*'s David French also sided with the Sith. Throwing various analogies against the wall, French declared that the Republic is "an insufferable European Union in space, a confederacy of preening elites," while the Jedi are "lightsaber-wielding jihadists of an intergalactic bureaucratic caliphate" seeking the annihilation of their ideological opponents, who "just" desire personal freedom.[6]

Conservatives in power have also celebrated the Empire. In the War on Terror, Dick Cheney announced that the United States would have to "work, though, sort of the dark side, if you will." The result was a secret program of abduction, torture and murder of suspects. Cheney came to embrace his reputation as Darth Vader. He even began using the Imperial March as his walk-up music for speeches.

In 2004, the journalist Ron Suskind recounted a conversation with an unnamed senior adviser to President George W. Bush. Characterizing hapless critics as being in the "reality-based community," the adviser (very much in Sith mode) declared that: "That's not the way the world really works anymore. We're an empire now, and when we act, we create reality...We're history's actors...and you, all of you, will be left to just study what we do."[7]

Donald Trump's former adviser and hard-right nationalist Steve Bannon echoed Cheney, declaring that: "Darkness is good...Dick Cheney. Darth Vader. Satan. That's power. It only helps us when [liberal critics] get it wrong. When they're blind to who we are and what we're doing."[8]

In response, Kate Aronoff suggests that, "The far right's Stormtrooper fixation might be turned to the Left's advantage... The moral lines of Star Wars' Empire-vs.-Rebel battle are nearly forty years old, and public opinion falls clearly on one side. If Trump's acolytes want to start favoring Imperial soldiers...on their heads be it."[9] But only if the rebellion does indeed take advantage as Aronoff suggests and starts telling stories that can counter the right's call to empire.

"The Rebellion Will Continue to Gain Support in the Imperial Senate"

If *Star Wars* was only a simple tale of good and evil, it wouldn't have needed the Empire. George Lucas could have just blended elements from myths, Japanese folktales and cinema, and Buck Rogers-style serials, and created an evil space wizard who needs to be defeated by the village hero. It would have worked well enough.

But *Star Wars* is political.[10] Its new left Rebels wouldn't have had anything to rebel against without the authoritarian militarism of the Empire. The rise of empire in our own world was also a reaction to being challenged by rebellion. As we'll see, it had to strike back.

As in the saga, we need to go back into history in order to understand the rise of empire. In many Western countries such as the US and the UK, after the Second World War a political consensus had developed, with some role for the state in managing the economy and running some major industries, and welfare states that provided a fair amount of security for citizens. It was like the Galactic Republic in *Star Wars*: an imperfect order, but better than the Old Republic that preceded it.

While the Galactic Republic afforded political representation to hundreds of worlds and star systems for the first time, much inequality and exploitation remained, particularly of the outlying Outer Rim territories compared to the central Core Worlds (including the Republic's capital of Coruscant). Like the Galactic Republic, our republics were what Marxists like to call bourgeois democracies, where freedoms exist but the fundamental beneficiaries are rich owners.

In our world, as in the saga, these tensions set in train the events leading to empire. As we've noted, this includes the social movements of the new left and their challenge to the republic. Alongside economic crises and trade union industrial action, this created a deep fear of increasing anarchy among many conservatives. Something had to be done. The first response to the new left and its new politics was a cultural backlash. Right-wing politicians such as Richard Nixon exploited the attitudinal gap between minority new left movements and the so-called "silent majority" of middle America (Ronald Reagan and Margaret Thatcher would later similarly claim to speak for this invented anti-progressive "middle"). In the words spoken by Palpatine at his Imperial Inauguration: "We are an Empire ruled by the majority! An Empire ruled by a new Constitution! An Empire of laws, not of politicians! An Empire devoted to the preservation of a just society. Of a safe and secure society!" But this call for order would not be enough.

"The Imperial Senate Will No Longer Be of Any Concern to Us"

Conservatives needed a more serious program of containment and control. As Mark Fisher suggests, the new right sought to crush the expanding forms of political and personal consciousness of the 1960s and 1970s by overthrowing the republic and replacing it with a new order.

Critics expressed bemusement that the first *Star Wars* prequel, *The Phantom Menace*, debuted with a dull dispute over the taxation of trade routes.[11] But George Lucas appears to understand how seemingly impenetrable economic crises can be used as a cover for dark political agendas. In the prequel trilogy, the secret society of anti-republican conspirators we know as the Sith create and exploit such a crisis. In our world, the new right seized on economic crises to claim that they had a political cause: the state having been captured by special interests and threatened by new social movements, and that the fundamental problem was democracy.

Like the Sith, the new right rejected the importance of balance. They desired to purge the republic of liberal and center-left ideas, such as a degree of government regulation of the economy, which they thought had "infected" conservative thinking. Most importantly, the new right's view that democracy allows the majority to violate the "liberty of the elite" meant that it needed to be pushed back.[12] (As Luke once said, "Amazing. Every word of what you just said was wrong.")

In place of the faltering republic, let alone the new left's hope for a new republic based on popular participation, the new right argued that politics could be replaced by a mysterious universal force: the free market. They claimed that this market is more democratic than politics could ever be. Consumers making their own decisions individually beats citizens making decisions together. But if the new order of markets should just be left alone, there is really nothing left for us to make decisions about.

Politics in any meaningful sense is over. From being democratic citizens, we become subjects of the market.

Many of these ideas and arguments were developed by think tanks, supposedly independent policy organizations that are often secretly funded by corporate interests. As Naomi Klein and others have pointed out, the new right's ideas were never very popular, hence why they had to be implemented first in dictatorships like Chile under Pinochet (Margaret Thatcher and Ronald Reagan were also fans). This wasn't fundamentally about economics. It was about eradicating opposition and capturing the state for the benefit of wealthy interests. It was about power.

"The Last Remnants of the Old Republic Have Been Swept Away"

Step-by-step, policies eroded our republics: deregulation, the privatization of nationalized industries, the reduction of welfare states and social security, restricting trade unions and increasing "flexibility" (reducing workers' rights) in labor markets. Within a generation, the new right had succeeded in changing the nature of politics, to the extent that by the 1990s the spectrum of permissible mainstream ideas within major political parties in countries like America and Britain encompassed only the marginal question of the extent of regulation that might help the market economy to operate more effectively. Empire was incontestable.

The effects have been disastrous. Corporate lobbying and campaign contributions have chipped away at policies and regulations that helped grow the middle class and strengthen the economy. Businesses have shipped millions of well-paying jobs overseas, exploiting desperate poverty around the world to erode employment protections and living standards at home. Chief executives receive huge bonuses for firing workers, closing plants and putting assets into the hands of ruthless speculators. Financial markets are casinos, while factories lie in ruins.

The manifest unfairness of these policies has fueled the public anger and disenchantment that today's hard right seizes on, but seeks to deflect the blame toward minorities and migrants. As Robert Kuttner suggests, it's not trade, immigration, globalization or technological change that are responsible for the harm to workers, it's global capitalism.[13] By limiting workers' rights, liberating bankers, allowing corporations to evade taxation and preventing nations from assuring economic security, raw capitalism strikes at the very foundation of a healthy democracy. The right used to argue that capitalism promotes democracy, but in fact democracy has expanded by limiting the power of capitalists. When that project fails, dark forces are unleashed.

As we noted in episode I, while the story told by the radical right may be deceitful, the lived experience its policies have led to is real. The Palpatines in our world have both created the crisis and seek to use the resulting chaos to their advantage. In the *Star Wars* prequels, the Trade Federation represents the greed and ambition of these political and business elites, which unchecked leads inexorably toward the death of democracy and the dawning of dictatorship.[14] As Nader Elhefnawy describes it:

Here we have a vast republic in which Big Business in its greed is trampling on everything and everyone, unrestrained by the government, which has had its courts and its legislators corrupted…Meanwhile, the most backward forms of exploitation and oppression continue to flourish – or perhaps, even resurge – at the margins (like slavery on Tatooine), and the whole system appears increasingly decrepit. Naturally the mess creates openings for reviving violent, irrational, reactionary elements (the Sith) that present themselves as partners to an economic elite determined not to compromise with the rest of society.[15]

If "politics" is only what benefits businesses (especially large corporations), then democracy has effectively been abolished, in principle if not totally in practice.[16] Why not just have corporations telling government what they want, a "capitalist democracy"? As Michael O'Connor notes:

> The Phantom Menace has the most blistering parody of this idea I've seen...In the Senate chamber, corporations like The Trade Federation and The Intergalactic Banking Clan aren't just lobbying for votes from Senate politicians. They have actual representation in the governing body. After all, if a corporation can be a person, why can't it be a politician as well?[17]

"What If I Told You That the Republic Was Now under the Control of a Dark Lord of the Sith?"

George Lucas incorporated plenty of references into the prequels about the corrosive effects of corporate capitalism on democracy. As noted by Jason Ward of *Making Star Wars*, while the OT dealt with imperialism and how a small band of people could rebel against a dominant establishment, the prequels were preoccupied with neoliberalism: the rise of corporate power and the turn toward imperialism that corrupts the republic.[18]

The principal villain of *The Phantom Menace* is the greedy Viceroy of the Trade Federation, Nute Gunray, whose name is a composite of new rightists Newt Gingrich and Ronald Reagan (flipped around to gun-ray). Halle Burtoni is the war profiteering alien in charge of manufacturing clone troopers for the Republic, a clear nod to Dick Cheney's former company Halliburton. The corporate corruption of the galaxy's governance is made clear. In *Attack of the Clones*, Queen Jamillia of the planet Naboo asks "The armies of commerce! Why has nothing been done in the Senate to restrain them?" Padmé responds that "I'm afraid that, despite the Chancellor's best efforts, there are still many bureaucrats, judges, and even Senators on the payrolls of the Guilds."

Most directly but missed by most commentators, in *Revenge of the Sith* Anakin Skywalker is forced to crash a space ship carrying the Supreme Chancellor into the planet's surface where the galaxy's government convenes. Soon after, the democratic Republic is reorganized into the totalitarian Empire. The ship is called the Invisible Hand, named after the term coined by the nineteenth-century economist Adam Smith – the notion that markets effectively organize themselves, a (false) idea so loved by today's neoliberals. As Jason Ward summarizes it: "When the Invisible Hand is brought to the galaxy's government, the galaxy willingly hands their democracy over to those that control capital accumulation. Although in the case of neoliberalism, it seems more sleight of hand is involved than invisible ones."[19]

Is this our future, or perhaps our present? As Wookieepedia (yes, that's a real thing) records what happened in the saga:

Ultimately, the Emperor preserved the Senate in order to make the Empire's member worlds believe that they still had a part to play in the government. Secretly, the Emperor planned to disband the Senate since the formation of the Empire in the proclamation of the New Order. But he needed its body to preserve order until the Death Star was completed, from which he could rule absolute through sheer terror. Some representatives, however, did not realize the extent of the Senate's powerlessness.[20]

Eventually, of course, as Grand Moff Tarkin informs his fellow space fascists in *A New Hope*: "I have just received word that the Emperor has dissolved the Council permanently." And with it the illusion of democracy in the galaxy. But as George Lucas reflected:

I grew up in the '60s. I grew up in San Francisco. And so I'm informed in a certain kind of way about, you know, believing in democracy and believing in America. And I'm a very ardent patriot. But I'm also a very ardent believer in democracy, not capitalist democracy. And I do not believe that the rich should be able to buy the government. And that's just the way I feel.[21]

"All His Life Has He Looked Away...to the Future, to the Horizon"

Beyond its impact on policy, the belief in the order of supposedly self-regulating markets has to some had the effect of abolishing the future, in the sense of our belief that we can choose any alternative futures we might dream of.

Famously, in the late 1980s and early 1990s, the political scientist Francis Fukuyama triumphantly declared the "end of history." This is the capitalist realism that Mark Fisher wrote about. The new right has argued, with considerable success, that capitalism is the only possible economic system (and one particular narrow hardline version of capitalism at that), and any other ways of organizing society are impossible. As a result, as Mark describes it, capitalism no longer necessarily presents itself as the best system among a range of alternatives, but as the only feasible one. Capitalist realism is an empire of the mind, or as Mark provocatively put it, the first successful totalitarian ideological system.

With the victory of the new right, the sociologist Zygmunt Bauman has noted the apparent paradox that: "If freedom has been won, how does it come about that human ability to imagine a better world and to do something to make it better was not among the trophies of victory?"[22]

But this book is about hope. Capitalist realism is more fragile than we often think. The Empire thought the Death Star was impregnable, after all, but the Rebels located its fundamental weakness (more than once).

"Fear Will Keep the Local Systems in Line"

Empire isn't just domestic. Indeed, one of the reasons we're told that capitalism is impregnable is because it is now so global.

There's been trade (and exploitation) between different countries for hundreds of years of course. But since the 1970s, "globalization" has referred to the increasing integration between countries due to greater trade across borders in goods and services, enabled by advances in transportation and communication technology. The new right's argument that you can't mess with markets seemed to fit with this new era in global trade: you have to be competitive, and that means adopting "pro-market" policies that support big businesses. Conform – or perish.

The global reach of entertainment products such as *Star Wars* can also be regarded as being a result of cultural globalization, the transmission of ideas, meanings and values around the world. Indeed, *Star Wars* was well-timed to exploit these trends just as they were accelerating and by its incorporation of universal myths.[23]

But as a Western cultural product, some critics have argued that the saga is imperialist in its racial attitudes and characterizations.[24] Others have suggested, quite the opposite, that in the human-supremacist Empire, *Star Wars* depicts the extension of power and dominion over other countries and cultures. Most obviously, the Galactic Empire, with its Star Destroyers and stiff-suited English actors, is the British imperial navy in space.[25]

Kevin J. Wetmore Jr. notes these themes running through the saga. The Empire represents the assertion of absolute power by a small group over a number of cultures through a combination of technology, capitalism and imperialism. Wetmore sees in the *Star Wars* films the use of technology that echoes nineteenth-century Europe's subjugation of parts of Africa, Asia, the Middle East, and Latin and South America, as well as an entire imperial organization dedicated to the direct administration of other peoples and cultures for the benefit of the center.[26]

But as discussed in the previous episode, the Empire is also contemporary America, something which M. Keith Booker emphasizes:

> The film's glorification of the rebels and their tactics carries a potentially subversive charge within the context of recent American history...[T]he Empire, with its vastly superior resources and technology, would seem to play the role in galactic politics that the United States now plays in world politics. Similarly, the under equipped but staunchly determined rebels...[resemble] the anticolonial fighters of the second half of the twentieth century and various Third World resistance movements of today, such as the Zapatistas of Mexico...[27]

Again though, some conservatives choose to celebrate empire. For example, the historian Niall Ferguson argues that British and American imperialism were on balance a "good thing" which made the world safe for a liberal political and economic order. His *Empire: How Britain Made the Modern World* doubts whether free markets can be achieved without empire, or as he provocatively puts it, "can you have globalization without gunboats?"[28] Freedom, Ferguson suggests, requires force.

The real subversiveness of *Star Wars* lies in dramatizing for a mass audience how a nation whose defining myths are anti-imperialism, freedom and self-determination is corrupted into becoming what it criticized – and further, how the only response is revolution.[29]

"Not Another Lecture, Master. Not on the Economics of Politics"

To Michael Hardt and Antonio Negri in their book *Empire* (2000), old-style imperialism has been replaced by a new type of empire. However, this may offer us hope.

Their book is a dense and abstract read ("Page-turners they were not," as Yoda would say). But the central argument is that globalization and the spread of capitalism are so pervasive that nation-states are no longer sovereign over their territories. As Slavoj Žižek points out, right-wing populism may not be correct, but it is a response to a real problem: that capitalism today is universal and Western capital is willing to sacrifice "first world" workers through outsourcing etc.[30] The new empire is more ubiquitous than its nineteenth century ancestors, and its forms of domination sometimes subtler. It is a universal order that accepts no boundaries or limits. Like the Galactic Empire, nothing exists outside it.

But this also means there is hope: "[T]he spectacle of imperial order is not an ironclad world, but actually opens up the real possibility of its overturning and new potentials for revolution."[31] Empire is so big, so all-encompassing, that it can't possibly control everything. Its global nature, the connections and exchanges of ideas and cultures it has led to, could form the basis for a truly democratic world society.

What the new right's version of capitalism has broken down – domestic politics, nation-states, local cultures – is what makes empire vulnerable to being overturned. It allows a rebel alliance – a diverse global web of workers, migrants, social movements and non-governmental organizations – to form and rise: "The creative forces of the multitude that sustain Empire are also capable of autonomously constructing a counter-Empire, an alternative political organization of global flows and exchanges."[32]

Paradoxically, the erosion of the idea of the collective mass, the previously hoped-for revolutionary industrial working class, means that each local struggle leaps immediately to the global level and strikes at the heart of empire.

Contrary to the pessimism of capitalist realism, empire, despite overflowing with power and wealth and seeming inescapable, may be surprisingly precarious. As we'll discuss in the next episode, it is facing a set of interlocking economic, ecological and energy crises. Its massive inequalities spur resistances from below, some reactionary and regressive, others, like the global justice and ecological movement, offering the potential of a just and free alternative.

"This Deal's Getting Worse"

The new right offered freedom from politics and liberty through markets. To paraphrase Lando Calrissian in *The Empire Strikes Back*, we thought we'd made a deal that would keep empire out of our lives forever. But for many, politics seems more inescapable than ever, and free markets feel like prisons.

Undoubtedly, capitalism can create new wealth and increase our capacity to produce goods and services. Even critics of capitalism such as Marxists acknowledge this, indeed it is central to their analysis of capitalism as a particular phase of (economic) history. At the same time, such critics see capitalism as increasingly prone to crises – crashes, conflicts and contradictions – that the system struggles to resolve.

The new right's arguments to renew capitalism as a force unleashed were an attempt to solve the crises it faced in the 1970s, including declining profits, increasing labor strikes and political protests. Some conservatives recognized the need to re-assert the power of capital (wealthy owners, big business, finance) against these threats. Their promise, their story, was that privatization, deregulation, labor market "flexibility," and tax cuts for the rich would benefit everyone through stronger economies. For a time, it appeared they were right. There did appear to be an economic boom in countries such as the US and UK, but alongside increasing unemployment and destructive change such as the rapid decline of manufacturing industry.

Here we are though, after nearly 40 years of the new right's empire: stagnant wages for the majority and greater job insecurity, lower taxes and tax evasion for the wealthy and big corporations, higher costs of living including health and housing costs for the rest of us, massively increased inequality, ballooning government and personal debt, and meager family savings and dwindling pensions.

But irrespective of its consequences, the imperial imperative is that new right market ideology needs to be imposed everywhere, on everything, with a consistent disregard or often deliberate destruction of any other values.

The idea of capitalist realism has abolished ideas about the future. But for many people, the new right's new capitalism has abolished their real futures. Under the republic of post-war Western capitalism, most working and middle-class people could plan for their own personal future as well as dream of a better collective future. Now, with permanent insecurity under the empire of the right, the future seems full of fear. The repeated response of employers, and the economic tenor of the times, is more like: "I am altering the deal. Pray I don't alter it any further."

"So This Is How Liberty Dies...with Thunderous Applause"

George Lucas was once asked what one thing he hoped fans understood about his films. He replied, "I only hope that those who have seen Star Wars recognize the Emperor when they see him."[33]

But why are we now surrounded by a new order of would-be and actual emperors, the likes of Trump, Erdoğan, Putin, Orbán, Duterte, Bolsonaro, and the rise of the far right more widely in many democracies? What happened to empire's promises of justice, safety and security?

When Palpatine is still a senator, he says, "The Republic is not what it once was. The Senate is full of greedy, squabbling delegates. There is no interest in the common good." He laments that, "The bureaucrats are in charge now." His campaign lie, of course, was to "Make the Republic Great Again," to drain the swamp of the Galactic Senate and serve the interests of the galaxy's citizens.

The new right has often relied on populism, even while its ideas were never that popular. It criticizes "liberal elites" as well as minorities, while transferring ever greater wealth and power to the real economic elite. But given the ever-tighter squeeze on people caused by new right policies, ever greater distractions are required. Or even better, from the new right's point of view, politics needs to be ever more tightly constrained, if not abolished altogether.

It seemed like a laughable title when it was first revealed, but *The Phantom Menace* points to Lucas's real interest in how would-be emperors seize power (through to *The Rise of Skywalker*, it's arguable that the saga is almost as much the story of empire as it is of rebellion). In the film, Palpatine secretly engineers the blockade of Naboo. The planet's (elected) Queen Amidala pleads in front of the Senate for help. When she is rejected, she calls for a vote of no confidence in Chancellor Velorum, leaving the way clear for Palpatine to replace him. But Naboo first had to feel surrounded and threatened.

George Lucas is often accused of being a bad writer, but as Cass Sunstein notices:

[The prequels] boldly don't do as the standard movie of this kind does, focus on individuals...[I]t's about institutions. And they have something to say about both how people go bad...especially about a little boy who loses his mother and then his loved one...And it's the threat of loss that gets to him...And there's something very similar that happens with the Republic. So, the institutional failure of a squabbling

legislature leading to interest in a strong paternal leader–
that's mirrored in the democratic process as it is in the
individual life.[34]

As we noted in episode I, loss is a powerful emotion that would-
be emperors exploit to manipulate people: a loss of security, of a
perceived past, of identity, meaning (as we also noted in episode
II, a similar sense of loss seems to motivate those conservative
fanboys who have turned against *Star Wars*). Emperors stoke
popular anger and turn it into rage to distract and disorientate
people, blame the marginalized and vulnerable, erode political
liberties and entrench themselves in power. They turn politics to
the dark side.

"Don't You Realize What's Going On?"

There are two fundamental debates among commentators and
political scientists about Trump and his fellow authoritarians:
whether they represent a break with new right thinking or its
next necessary stage; and whether they are fascists.

To the first question, the new right's ideas lead to authoritarian
politics for the simple reason that these ideas don't deliver what
they promised. Nor are they really meant to. The old republic
of capitalism was based on the simple notion that at least some
of the wealth generated by workers needed to go back to them,
to buy goods and services. No consumers means no wealth and
power for the rich. Our Sith, the new right, seem to think that
this represents an unnecessary compromise.

As discussed, this is because new right ideas are not about
freedom, but control. As Mark Fisher notes, because it is
fundamentally a political strategy rather than an economic one,
the new right will always put political goals above economic
ones. This is why, for example, they have created massively more
unequal societies that entrench the power of the wealthy and
corporations, but paradoxically to the extent that this generates

such immiseration and public anger that it begins to threaten the system as a whole.

Enter the would-be emperors, to distract and disorientate, to finish the job of concentrating power in the hands of the few, through the use of exaggerated threats and dangers, of warning about the "enemies of the people" within and without. We've seen how this works, in fact and fiction. Like Trump, like Palpatine.

To the second question, the fascist style is certainly present.[35] Trump, for example, engages in rhetorical violence against groups opposing him or associated with his opponents, including protestors, immigrants, Muslims, minorities, the mainstream media, judges, investigators...Prominent Democrats and media outlets have been targeted by right-wing terrorists, who are now the greatest security threat in the United States.[36] He has emboldened the far right, who recognize him as one of their own. Other emperors order the assassination of political opponents.

But as Naomi Klein emphasizes in *No Is Not Enough*, Trump is not a rupture but rather the logical culmination of many dangerous stories our culture has been telling for a very long time.[37] These are stories of admiration for extreme wealth, economic and environmental exploitation, waging imperial wars, bullying, the legitimacy of sexism and racism, and scaremongering and scapegoating. Trump's marriage of corporate elitism and far-right authoritarianism makes perfect sense. It's the Sith reveling in being able to reveal themselves at last.

"You're Confusing Peace with Terror"
As George Lucas comments:

All democracies turn into dictatorships – but not by coup. The people give their democracy to a dictator, whether it's Julius Caesar or Napoleon or Adolf Hitler. Ultimately, the general population goes along with the idea. What kinds of things push people and institutions in this direction? That's the issue I've been exploring.[38]

It's not that Lucas presents the Republic as perfect. Its corrosion and collapse demonstrate its weaknesses. It was riddled with corruption. It was decadent, as emphasized by the luxurious digital production design of the prequels. Its democracy was sclerotic.[39] Its protectors, the Jedi, were complacent, distracted, disinterested in inequality and injustice, and ultimately outmaneuvered. *The Washington Post's* Dan Drezner characterizes the Jedi as sensible centrists, intent on moderating power and keeping peace, but failing to recognize the threat the Republic faces until it is too late.[40] The Jedi Code of non-attachment also makes them resemble technocratic elitists who fail to recognize the importance of emotion and identity in the galaxy's politics.

Hannah Arendt would have told Lucas (and perhaps he would agree) that the population "goes along" with authoritarianism because representative democracy is too limited:

The success of totalitarian movements among the masses meant the end of two illusions of democratically ruled countries...The first was that the people in its majority had taken an active part in government...On the contrary...a democracy could function according to rules which are actively recognized by only a minority. The second democratic illusion...was that these politically indifferent masses did not matter, that they were truly neutral and constituted no more than the inarticulate backward setting for the political life of the nation.[41]

In the Empire, Lucas deliberately demonstrates the appeal of authoritarianism. Will Brooker suggests that Lucas was attracted to both sides of the galactic civil war, the coldly organized aesthetic of the Empire and the raw improvisation of the Rebels. Whether this is accurate psychologically, it's not true politically. Nowhere in the films or any other media are we given the sense that the Empire delivers any actual benefits for the galaxy's citizens. Nonetheless, authoritarianism draws on people's widespread sense of exclusion from decision-making. It offers, falsely, the power and control people feel they lack.

"Power! Unlimited Power!"

Ultimately, the Emperor declares to the Senate: "In order to ensure our security and continuing stability, the Republic will be reorganized into the first Galactic Empire, for a safe and secure society which I assure you will last for ten thousand years." In our world, fascism now presents a more virulent threat to peace and justice than at any time since its defeat at the end of the Second World War. The momentum toward democracy has been thrown into reverse.

The left has been accused of crying wolf about fascism, cheapening its meaning by reducing it to a generalized term of abuse for opponents, even seeing it in mass popular culture. But in the story, the wolf does eventually arrive. In its fantastical way, *Star Wars* might help mass audiences see what fascism is and how it seizes power – its manipulations, fear-mongering, violence, annihilation of political opponents, its rampant self-interest and corrosive corruption.

In the original and sequel trilogy, the fascists are clearly characterized in black and white terms. But as Mark Eldridge notes, despite their reputation the prequels better illustrate the conditions that help fascism's rise to power: a flawed and arrogant elite, politicians riddled with corruption, owned by corporations and ultimately overtaken by an evil cult.[42]

But fascism is also a story, one that needs to be fought with better stories. Fascists exploit the near-universal desire to be part of a meaningful quest. The answer to fascism is more democracy, returning prosperity, security and power to ordinary people, and fundamentally, engaging millions of people in a collective meaningful quest, a rebellion that restores peace, justice and real security to the world.

Or else, as we have been warned, "Fear is the path to the dark side. Fear leads to anger, anger leads to hate, hate leads to suffering."

"The Death Star Will Be in Range in Five Minutes"

"No Star System Will Dare Oppose the Emperor Now"

Why did the Empire keep building Death Stars?[1] This is repetitive storytelling, even for a series known for its many rhymes. But it's difficult to think of a much better plot device in popular film than the Death Star: a massive ticking time bomb that must be destroyed or all hope will be lost. It also makes sense as an embodiment of Imperial thinking: the overriding belief in technology, particularly its use for war and violence, and mechanistically doing the same thing again and again until you dominate everything.[2]

It was also about fear and intimidation of course. With Grand Moff Tarkin (the overseer of the station), the Emperor designed the Death Star as the ultimate deterrent, enabling the Empire to control the left behind Outer Rim territories through fear of reprisals.[3] This could have been achieved through normal military means, but as its name suggests the Death Star was about destroying all hope of defeating the Empire. It was designed to induce defeatism.

From its first appearance, the Death Star lodged in our collective imagination as a symbol for epic destructive capabilities and for the fearful, twisted minds that conceive of such machines. As such, it's a pretty good metaphor for an oppressive, exploitative, crisis-ridden contemporary capitalism that left unchecked seems destined to destroy us.

This episode is a bit like *The Empire Strikes Back*. It's a bit of a downer, with problem after problem, and the forces against us seem insurmountable (then again, *Empire* is many fans' favorite film). Neoliberal economics is a system of control which is squeezing people harder and harder, a totalizing regime which is always demanding more and granting less in return. This is *empirism* – the Sith-like drive for ever-increasing domination and exploitation. Rather than ensuring order and security, its ever-encroaching consumption of people and resources is creating chaos and disorder, and threatens our existence on a planetary scale.

And yet, empire's plans have a key structural weakness. Fear and control are not the solutions, they're the fundamental problem. The only answer is destroying that which threatens to destroy us. As Jyn Erso says in *Rogue One*: "What chance do we have? The question is what choice?"

"We Have Them Tied on the End of a String"

As we've discussed, despite being a democracy the Galactic Republic was highly unequal, dominated by the wealthy who looked away from rampant exploitation and slavery. Huge disparities in resources and power existed between developed and undeveloped worlds. The Empire drew on widespread frustrations to entrench control in its own evil elite.

We mentioned in the previous episode the effects of 40 years of the new right's empire. It's true that absolute poverty globally has decreased over the past few decades. But 700 million people still endure extreme poverty, and malnutrition and undernutrition cause 3.1 million deaths every year. Further, due to climate change, hunger and food insecurity are increasing for the first time in 15 years, all the while that *the world's 26 richest people own the same wealth as the poorest half of humanity*.[4] There is an elite, but they are not the cultural Marxism-spreading college professors of the right's vivid imagination.

And slavery still exists in our world. Today's slave labor mostly involves poor people in developing countries being exploited in clothing and shoe factories. Across the world,

25 million people are victims of forced labor. Most of them are exploited by companies for profit rather than by private individuals.[5]

Inequality within many countries has also increased. This is partly a result of globalization, or rather the neoliberal model of globalization. Between 1980 and 2010, competition for low- and medium-skill jobs went global, contributing to the polarization of employment and wages in developed economies. Across 25 developed economies, 65-70 percent of households (540-580 million people) saw their real incomes stay flat or fall in the decade 2005-2014. The figures for the US and UK are 81 and 70 percent of households respectively.[6]

Empire is squeezing harder. Middle-class life in developed countries is not coming back. The new poverty is working poverty, with stagnant wages, precarious employment, zero hours contracts and reduced or nonexistent benefits.[7] In the US, for example, this has had a number of disastrous effects. People are drowning in debt. Personal bankruptcy has gone from a rare occurrence to a relatively common one. Americans have been losing their homes at record rates through foreclosure and evictions. Millions of families have virtually no accumulated wealth to tide them over when things go wrong.[8]

No wonder this is affecting people's health. In the US, life expectancy is falling for some groups. Increasing unemployment of non-college whites in the past 2 decades, driven by automation and outsourcing, may have contributed to rising morbidity rates.[9]

We are creating the perfect environment for empire's authoritarians. And it will get worse.

"This Party's Over"

Increasing inequality, poor education, an aging population and rising debt will hold back productivity growth. We have entered a new "age of stagnation."[10] As a result, over the next few decades economic growth is predicted to be much lower than in the past. In the past, rapid population growth and increases in labor productivity have driven increases in gross domestic product (GDP). Now, slower population growth, longer life expectancy and aging populations are slowing growth or even reducing the working-age population. Even if productivity were to increase at the same annual rate as the past half-century, over the next 50 years GDP growth in developed and emerging economies will still decrease by 40 percent and GDP growth per person by almost 20 percent. Even worse, if the low economic growth of the past decade continues, over the next decade 70 to 80 percent of households will experience flat or falling incomes.[11]

This will mean even more income inequality; it is projected to increase by more than 30 percent in OECD (richer) countries and by 20 percent in the other G20 (biggest) economies until 2060.[12] Nearly all of this widening inequality will be between high and medium earners, due to technology increasingly replacing medium-skilled jobs. The average OECD country could face the same level of inequality as today's US. All this at the same time as government debt in the developed world has reached a 200-year high.[13] This debt is unlikely to be reduced in an era of lower growth and aging populations.

Further, none of these long-term projections include other risks that could affect government finances in the future, such as wars, financial shocks or climate crises.

"He's More Machine Now than Man"

In episode III, we mentioned the Empire's attachment to technology for colonization and domination. Marx described how, as a result of how work is organized and the extensive use of machinery, our labor has lost its individual character. We become appendages to machines, controlled by the process of production instead of controlling it. He called this alienation.

The most obvious analogy in *Star Wars* is Darth Vader, who

embodies an estrangement from any authentic self, an unearthly interface between a damaged humanity and technological life support. As Canaan Perry suggests, the Empire is similarly subsumed by its own technological constructions, whereas the Rebels use and adapt technology but are not slaves to it.[14]

Technology is set to dominate our lives in the future even more than it does now. Like the difference between the Empire and Rebels, whether it enslaves or frees us depends on in whose interests it is used. Automation and artificial intelligence (AI) could liberate us from work and provide a better standard of living for everybody. But in the hands of empire they will mainly be used to benefit corporations and increase inequality.[15] A widely-cited 2013 study of more than 700 occupations by researchers at the University of Oxford found that 47 percent of all jobs in the US (more than 60 million jobs) are at risk of being fully automated over the next 20 years.[16] Globally, by 2030 between 400 million and 800 million people could need to find new jobs as a result of automation.[17]

As the American sociologist Randall Collins suggests, in the past capitalism has escaped from its own "technological displacement crisis" (technology eradicating jobs and eroding middle-class wealth) by using it to create new jobs and industries, spreading markets to new geographical areas, relying on the financial sector, increasing government employment or soaking up unemployment by expanding education. None of these options now offers an escape route: AI won't create sufficient jobs, capitalism is already global, financialization creates even more volatility and governments no longer have the resources to save capitalism from itself.[18] As Lando says in *Solo*, "You might want to buckle up, baby."

"If there's a Bright Center to the Universe, You're on the Planet It's Farthest From"

Globally, there are 1.8 billion young people between the ages of 10 and 24 – the largest youth population ever. Nine in ten of them live in developing countries. Yet young people are three times more likely to be unemployed than adults. Over 70 million young people are out of work – more than 35 percent of the unemployed population globally. With low pay, more than 40 percent of the world's youth is either unemployed or living in poverty despite being employed. This is one of the worst, if not the worst, youth unemployment crises in history.[19]

Developed economies are also struggling to provide good employment for young people. Lower growth, job insecurity and a lack of relevant skills and experience have created fewer opportunities for security for younger generations. In the US, millennials' median household income is lower than previous generations.[20] They have a record $1.5 trillion in student loan debt. The proportion who own houses is at an historic low. In real terms, average hourly earnings peaked well before they were born.[21] They may be the first generation for whom average life expectancy falls.

As a result of insecure work, lower pay, eroding social security and pensions, more than half of current workers in the US are destined to retire without saving enough to maintain their standard of living in old age.[22] It might not be surprising then that there is widespread pessimism across many developed countries about whether young people will enjoy better prospects than their parents' generation.

"If They Knew What We Were Trying to Build Here, They'd Destroy Us"

As Nick Srnicek has described it, the fundamental foundations of the economy are rapidly being carved up among a small number of monopolistic digital platforms, dubbed "platform capitalism."[23] The Sarlaac Pits of this new economy are companies like Facebook, Amazon, Apple, Netflix and Google, suitably known as the FAANGs. They are imperial in their design, dependent on insatiable growth to seize and consolidate monopoly power. Facebook wants to monopolize (social) media, Google all search (really, all knowledge), Amazon all (online) commerce.

More broadly, we are being monopolized. Amazon is one of five corporations that dominate the economy, shaping how we shop and the prices we pay. It has eviscerated brick-and-mortar retailers, broken unionization efforts, tried to crush the publishing industry and even offered its facial recognition technology to the US Immigration and Customs Enforcement agency.

Welcome to the age of "surveillance capitalism." As Shoshana Zuboff describes it, this is the latest phase in capitalism's long evolution – from making products, to mass production, managerial capitalism, through services to financial capitalism, and now to the exploitation of behavioral predictions covertly derived from the surveillance of users offered "free" products.[24]

These corporations monopolize data science and dominate machine intelligence, as well as their ecosystems of suppliers and customers, and our channels for social participation. They also have vast capital reserves. As Shoshana suggests, whereas most democratic societies have at least some degree of oversight of state surveillance, we currently have almost no regulatory oversight of its privatized counterpart. Like any empirists, the first surveillance capitalists conquered by declaration: they simply declared our private experiences to be theirs for the taking.

What if such tools fell into the wrong hands? They already have. As the whistleblower Christopher Wylie, formerly director of research at Cambridge Analytica, has said, tech companies are colonizing society. Facebook is our generation's East India Company. And they've facilitated the rise of the hard right: "When you look at what the alt-right is and what the role of Cambridge Analytica was in catalyzing the alt-right – it's an insurgency. It was built to be an insurgency. People who were vulnerable to disinformation were profiled and targeted using the same kinds of techniques and tactics the military would use against ISIS."[25]

No wonder many of us feel that we are being menaced by phantom forces. No wonder we listen when someone promises, "Only I can bring order"...

"I Thought We Were in Trouble There for a Second"

Not unrelatedly, since the mid-2000s we have also been in a global democratic recession, a term coined by Larry Diamond, a political scientist at Stanford University. But this implies a temporary slump. It's worse: it's a depression.

The US organization Freedom House's annual report found that 2018 was the thirteenth consecutive year of deteriorating freedoms around the globe.[26] Since 2006, 116 countries have seen a decline, while only 63 countries have experienced improvement. We've seen the incremental weakening of democracy in many emerging countries, the deepening of authoritarianism in non-democracies and decline in the functioning of established democracies alongside the growth of hard-right forces. Similarly, the *2018 World Press Freedom Index* compiled by Reporters Without Borders reveals an increase in the number of countries where media freedom is very weak.[27] It has worsened in nearly two-thirds of the 180 countries in the Index.

According to political scientists, behind this is the sense of threat felt by an increasing number of voters about how their societies are changing, of diversity and complexity, and a strong desire for order and unity. Of course, these feelings are also manufactured and manipulated by authoritarians – and they are winning. As democrats, we need to listen to people, but not the impulse to undermine democracy. As Yoda says, "Dangerous and disturbing this puzzle is."

"I've Never Had the Luxury of Political Opinions"

Just when we need existing political institutions to lead us through these challenges, public trust is in long-term decline. Across developed countries just 42 percent of citizens have confidence in their national government.[28] At no point in the last 4 decades have Americans expressed less trust in their political leaders than they do today – only 18 percent, a near historic low. The figure for millennials is similar, at 20 percent.[29]

Although, as we'll see, many young people are engaging in politics, a lot of them are also disengaged because they don't trust mainstream politics. American millennials may now be the largest generation in the electorate but more than a quarter of them aren't registered to vote, more than a third didn't vote in the 2016 Presidential election, and 70 percent don't consider themselves to be politically engaged or active.[30] And yet, more than half of them think that the country is heading in the wrong direction, and two-thirds say they are fearful about the future of their democracy. Forty-three percent think that politics is no longer able to meet the challenges the country is facing, and they mainly blame politicians and money in politics.[31]

The OECD notes three major "pressure points" by which public trust is being lost: concern about economic growth and jobs and its impact on income and inequality; anger over persistent problems of corruption, tax evasion, and other signs of a lack of respect for the rule of law; and lack of belief in the ability of governments to manage global pressures and risks such as climate change, geopolitical conflict, terrorism and large-scale migration.[32] Rising inequality in particular appears to be undermining trust in government and democratic institutions. Countries with higher income inequality have lower support for democracy.[33] Inequality is also correlated with falling trust in others.[34] This is how republics fall.

"We're Doomed!"

The greatest crisis we face is of course climate change and environmental destruction.

In 2009, an international group of experts identified nine interconnected "planetary boundaries" that underpin the stability of the global ecosystem.[35] Three boundaries have already been passed (climate change, biodiversity and the nitrogen cycle) and two are coming close to being passed (ocean acidification and the phosphorus cycle).[36] Worse, all of the trends are speeding-up, a "great acceleration" beyond environmental limits. We are Alderaan. The difference is we are destroying ourselves.

The 20 warmest years since records began have been in the past 22 years. Since 1950, the number of floods has increased by a factor of 15, extreme temperature events by a factor of 20 and wildfires sevenfold. We know that seas will rise, cities will be flooded and some will become too hot to live in. But we are also in the midst of a man-made extinction. Vertebrate populations have fallen by an average of 60 percent since the 1970s. Insect numbers vital for pollination have declined even faster in some countries. A quarter of all mammals, a fifth of all reptiles, and a sixth of all birds are heading toward oblivion. Flora and fauna loss by the end of the twenty-first century could be between 20 and 50 percent of all species on earth.[37]

This will destroy our own means of survival; food systems that rely on just five animal and 12 plant species provide three-quarters of the world's nutrition. Feeding the world's projected population in 2050 will require a 70 percent increase in food production.[38] Constantly increasing yields from major crops is unrealistic, raising alarm about "peak food." Over 1.3 billion people are already trapped on degrading agricultural land.[39]

At the same time, water insecurity will be one of the greatest challenges of the twenty-first century. In 2000, 500 million people lived in countries chronically short of water; by 2050 this will increase to more than 4 billion.[40] As climate change also increases the frequency of extreme weather events, a "one-in-100-year" shock to global food production may become three times more likely by the middle of this century.[41] Maybe Alderaan is not the best analogy; more likely we're creating Tatooine – a formerly lush planet of forests and oceans, now a baking, barren, brutal desert.

"That Is the Sound of a Thousand Terrible Things Headed This Way"

Scarcity feeds insecurity. From Africa to Asia and Latin America, the era of climate wars has begun; extreme weather is bringing banditry, humanitarian crisis and state failure.[42] According to UNHCR, the United Nations Refugee Agency, there were 65.6 million forced migrants in 2017 – refugees and internally displaced people, from conflicts, environmental disasters and famine. This is the highest level of people displaced by violence and persecution since the Second World War.

Mass migration and refugees will continue to increase. The climate crisis could lead to ten times more refugees from the Middle East than the 12 million who fled during the past few years of upheaval and turmoil. The hard right has skillfully manipulated and inflamed a backlash over this crisis. By denying climate change and blocking action, they will make mass forced migration more likely and then reap the benefits by whipping up hatred against the tide of human misery.

We have crossed over a threshold into an age of systemic risk, in which population pressures, natural resources, climate, politics and the economy will interact in predictable and unpredictable ways to create global crises which feed on and magnify each other. It is a crisis of crises, what James Howard Kunstler has called the "long emergency."[43]

Empire has got us to this point: a highly interdependent and networked world, in which even local events can have substantial repercussions in distant regions through technological and financial networks, trade flows, migration, public health crises and environmental disasters. Far from ensuring peace and security, we are increasingly exposed to major risks.

This emergency is also the greatest form of intergenerational inequality the world has ever seen. A much warmer world is one with floods, droughts, drowned cities and coastlines, crop failures, unprecedented levels of mass migration, and conflict – all of it arriving for the next generation.

"Don't Be Too Proud of This Technological Terror You've Constructed"

One of George Lucas's obsessions running through the saga is how greed and fear lead to the dark side – they *are* the dark side, an all-consuming hunger and acquisitiveness, born of a driving anxiety of loss and losing, that leads to personal and political corruption.

We face many crises, but really it is just one crisis. At root it is not economic or political but philosophical and psychological. It is empirism: the compulsion to dominate people, nature and thought. It's the Sith's individualistic "morality" of acquisition.[44]

Beneath this way of seeing the world is the idea of separation. To Charles Eisenstein (*Climate, A New Story*), the essence of this is the notion of a separate self in a world of "other." It is a zero-sum mentality that the more control we exercise over others and nature, the better off we will be: "Our destiny, then, is to ascend beyond nature's original limits, to become its lords and masters."[45] Similarly, to Rebecca Solnit, behind the denial or acquiescence about climate change is a white supremacist ideology of separation, that "we" will be okay even if others are suffering gravely, and a refusal to recognize that our actions have consequences.[46]

Empirism has always been at the core of industrial capitalism, its exploitation of labor, natural "resources," indigenous lands, need for continual growth and expansion, and its extraction of vast wealth and power for the few while draining the natural wealth of "our" planet. As campaigner and activist Charles Derber (*Welcome to the Revolution*) puts it, in earlier centuries capitalism freed millions from ancient forms of bondage and want. Today's capitalism creates and perpetuates isolation and insecurity, extreme inequality, corporate power, billionaire rule, militarism, repression, climate change, environmental destruction and exclusion.[47]

Part of the reason that capitalism has become so universal is technology. Our Death Star, a technology-driven nuclear concentration of economic and political power, has already been built. It was built 40 years ago in the new right revolution: a turbo-charged, no limits, corporate-dominated global capitalism. But as Denis Wood identifies:

The deepest question posed by Star Wars is the extent to which an organism or organization can exploit others as technologic extensions of its own system of intentions. Thorough technocrats recognize no limits: everything can be legitimately employed as extensions of their own will. The Imperials are in this sense...unredeemably technocrats, complete fascists. To achieve their ends, or, technocratically, to solve their problems, the Imperials can use, and use up, anything.[48]

This is reaching its end. Limitless extraction and growth are not possible on a finite planet. As Yuval Harari notes, our profound dilemma is that: "[E]conomic growth will not save the global ecosystem – just the opposite, it is the cause of the ecological crisis. And economic growth will not save the technological disruption – it is predicated on the invention of more and more disruptive technologies."[49]

As Charles Eisenstein suggests, the changes we need are far more profound than "merely" switching our industrial societies to zero carbon energy; every aspect of our societies needs to come into alignment with a new story of "interbeing," that who I am and who I am able to be depends on who you are, and what happens to the world is in some ways also happening to me. "Search your feelings, you know it to be true!"

"Everything Is Proceeding as I Have Foreseen"

It would be a fatal mistake to assume that, as these crises concentrate, the left will naturally benefit in order to make the radical changes necessary – that, to quote Nute Gunray, "In time, the suffering of your people will persuade you to see our point of view."

Automation will destroy millions of jobs. A floating surplus population will be used as a threat against those "lucky" enough to still be working in increasingly low-paying roles requiring human input.[50] Racial and geographical disparities will intensify, while the global financial class consolidates its power. Climate and environmental crisis will cause spiraling conflicts. National borders will rise higher to control the flow of populations and force more migrant workers to live outside of the law.

There's a reason why the Sith love war and conflict. This is how empire will exacerbate and exploit these crises, directing fear and frustration into support for authoritarianism.[51] Naomi Klein has described "disaster capitalism" as the use of shock events, natural disasters and terror attacks to advance the free-market economic revolution, which destroys the myth of the new right's supposedly peaceful global victory and the supposed link between freedom and capitalism.[52] But the economic system is now one big crisis. All capitalism is disaster capitalism.

"The World Is Coming Apart"

As Naomi Oreskes and Erik Conway note in *The Collapse of Western Civilization: A View from the Future*, because of the crises it creates, neoliberalism is more likely to lead to large-scale government intervention, and not a progressive version either. It will be to protect the rich from the chaos and to police the disorder.[53]

In the twentieth century, capitalism coexisted quite happily with dictatorships, which tend to create "business friendly" environments and repress worker organizations.[54] Western capitalists have also enriched despots in the developing world who crush local democracy. In the West, big business is happy for right-wing administrations to burn regulations and slash taxes, looking in other directions to the assaults on democracy, voting rights, anti-discrimination laws and immigrant rights.[55]

Welcome to the new fascism. As Antonio Negri analyses it, it attempts to promote a "more neoliberal development of the deep crisis...the force of authoritarianism is called up to sustain the crisis of liberalism...Having dislocated or rejected the old democratic constitutional equilibrium, now it is exposed to the void."[56]

Consequently, as Peter Frase in *Four Futures, Life After Capitalism* suggests, without radical change our most likely future is "exterminism," a neo-feudal nightmare in which the rich retreat to heavily fortified enclaves where the robots do all the work and everyone else is trapped outside in the hot, soggy hell of a rapidly warming planet (or perhaps warehoused in prisons and refugee camps).[57]

The new right's ideas have not delivered order and security, quite the opposite. But that is precisely why they are winning. Just as Palpatine/Sideous created and exploited a crisis to advance authoritarianism, so our Sith use the crises they have created to finish what they started. Like its fictional equivalent, through the crises it creates, empire appears quite happy to kill millions of people to hold onto power. "Wipe them out. All of them," as the Emperor said.

"In a Dark Place We Find Ourselves"

No wonder the generation that needs to change the world is increasingly anxious and depressed.

In *How Will Capitalism End?*, the German sociologist Wolfgang Streeck provides an ethnography of everyday life under post-crash Western capitalism.[58] Burdened by debt, unlikely ever to get a decent pay rise and resigned to the erosion of the public sphere through cuts, Streeck describes many of us as "coping, hoping, doping and shopping."

It isn't working. Depression is now the leading cause of disability worldwide. In the US, 40 million adults (18 percent of the population) suffer from anxiety disorders each year, the most common mental illness.[59] In particular, there has been a significant rise in mental health issues among young people, to the highest levels ever recorded. Anxiety affects a quarter of young people between 13 and 18 years old. In the UK, more than 60 percent of young people regularly feel stressed and more than a quarter say they often feel hopeless.[60] Forty percent don't feel in control of their lives. Nearly half have experienced a mental health problem. Even more alarmingly, nearly one in five (18 percent) don't think life is worth living.[61] In a survey of 20 countries, British youth had the poorest mental wellbeing in the world, second only to Japan.[62]

Globally, this is a generation that seems deeply pessimistic about the future. More than a third are convinced that the world is getting worse, while just 20 percent think it is getting better (young people in developing countries are more positive). They worry about extremism, terrorism and conflict, increasing inequality, lack of access to education, climate change, global pandemics and the pace of technological change including their jobs being automated.

In *Capitalist Realism*, Mark Fisher points to several ways in which capitalism is detrimental to our mental wellbeing, including job insecurity, the toll of overwork on families, the envy and inadequacy stoked by advertising, and economic hardship and its equation with personal failure. As Mark suggested, we need to ask how it has become acceptable that so many people, especially young people, are ill. Rather than being the only system that works and somehow "natural," capitalism seems inherently dysfunctional, including to human wellbeing.

As Shoshana Zuboff says, the big contradiction at the heart of contemporary capitalism is that we are promised control over our own lives, but everywhere it is thwarted by rising inequality, exclusion, pervasive competition and degrading social and economic stratification.[63] This lack of control is closely correlated with mental illness.

Today's young people have also grown up with crisis: financial crashes, terror attacks, political instability, rising xenophobia and authoritarianism (as noted, the *Star Wars* prequels anticipate this era of threats and fears, manipulation and misinformation, militarization and creeping restrictions on civil liberties). It's easy for old media to blame social media for young people's anxiety, but this is to ignore the bigger reasons for the mental illness epidemic. As the meme has it, "It's not you, it's capitalism." To Dave Schilling, there's also an echo of young people's pessimism in the most recent *Star Wars* films:

> People my age, the dreaded "'90s kids" who grew up with the worst Star Wars movies – the cursed prequels – look back at the promise of post-war America with a mixture of contempt and jealousy. You promised us a better tomorrow and we got terrorism, massive income inequality, the threat of nuclear war, political instability throughout the globe, and whatever devastation climate change will bring. Similarly, Luke, Leia, Han, and the Rebel Alliance promised a new Republic and a return to decency in the galaxy...Our new characters, particularly Rey and Kylo Ren, find themselves questioning the value of all that hope.[64]

"I Sense Much Fear in You"

We face the grave danger of more young people turning to the dark side. *Star Wars* has its share of characters struggling to find their identities. They are experiencing a tumultuous galactic civil war after all, so it's not surprising that they manifest all sorts of psychological conditions.[65] How they cope is one of the reasons the saga is compelling to so many people, especially because our rebel heroes still find ways to display courage, compassion and hope (Carrie Fisher was loved not just as an actress and writer but also as an advocate and campaigner for mental health). Others, however, succumb to the Sith.

In *Attack of the Clones*, Anakin suggests that the Galactic Senate should be made to resolve its differences by "Someone wise." Padmé responds, "That sounds an awful lot like a dictatorship to me." "Well, if it works…," Anakin counters. Later, Anakin's personal fear of loss and lack of control leaves him prey to Palpatine's perfidious plot.

Reviewing the film, Michael Sragow suggests that, "…[A]ll along, Lucas intended to create a series that would demonstrate the seductiveness of fascism to boys like Anakin, who are disgusted with the compromises of a weak, degraded democracy, as well as depict the formation of a totalitarian style."[66] As Michael notes, Anakin's rebellion takes reactionary form: he chafes at lectures from naive do-gooders and is drawn instead toward a worldly-wise counselor who offers him a solution to his pain and confusion…

In the sequel films, the Vader cosplaying Kylo Ren is not so much seduced into the Sith as much as dives into the dark side in order to act out his power fantasies. No wonder the alt-right doesn't like the new *Star Wars*. Ren captures their adolescent attention-seeking shock tactics perfectly. Han is right when says to Ren that "[Snoke]'s only using you for your power." Depressed, alienated, sometimes desperate young men (it is young men, typically) are being led toward fascism by facile father figures. But as Martin Winiecki argues, what's really going on is about capitalism.[67] The economic system has corralled us into monotonous, meaningless jobs, and when we struggle to succeed, labels us losers ("My disappointment in your performance cannot be overstated," as Snoke says). In such conditions of anxiety, mistrust and violence, authoritarianism always looms, especially when economic structures crumble and charismatic leaders channel suppressed emotions and exploit them to give free rein to corporations. The people most attracted to fascism can also find a certain status in it: others finally fear them.

As Hannah Arendt suggested, especially in *The Origins of Totalitarianism*, fascism is everywhere rooted in dehumanization: first the loss of dignity we feel ourselves by being left behind by capitalism, then our dehumanization of others in reaction. The preconditions for domination are individual isolation and loneliness. Indeed, Arendt called totalitarianism a kind of organized loneliness.

Rather than allowing more young people to slip into the waiting arms of the First Order, we need to provide them with a different grand narrative, one that gives their lives meaning and purpose. We need to persuade them that, given everything that protesting and campaigning and struggle has achieved in history, "A thousand generations live in you now…but this is your fight."

"Stopped They Must Be. On This All Depends"
As George Lucas reflected: "One day Princess Leia and her friends woke up and said, 'This isn't the Republic anymore, it's the Empire. We are the bad guys. Well, we don't agree with this. This democracy is a sham, it's all wrong.'"[68]

Lucas has never been a socialist or communist. *Star Wars* is what it is because he was living through revolutionary times in which young people were faced with a choice between two sides, empire and rebels. But this makes his story all the more effective: a call for rebellion from a mainstream liberal guy in extraordinary circumstances.

We talk about "radical politics." But as the actor and activist Ellen Page says, "We need to stop claiming the political activists are 'radical.' The people who are fucking radical are the people who want to keep destroying our water and our top soil and our air in order to give a few people billions more dollars."[69] Empirists are the real extremists. Being radical is now the only way to be responsible.

We face a planet-destroying empire – ideologically-driven, deceptive and dangerous. Our most likely path is toward the dark side: violent, exploitative, racist and authoritarian. Unless we change course, unless we rebel against the system that's leading us there. And who is the rebellion? It's whoever realizes we can't go on like this, that compromise and accommodation and conciliation with empire is no longer possible. As Michael J. Hanson says, the Rebel Alliance represents the will of the people not to tolerate a life of fear.[70]

There isn't much time. We need to act, as our favorite Rebels did.

"That's How We're Gonna Win. Not Fighting What We Hate, but Saving What We Love"

"People Are Counting on Us. The Galaxy Is Counting on Us"

We know what they were against, but what were the Rebels *for*?

Their proper name was the Alliance to Restore the Republic. As their Formal Declaration of Rebellion suggests, the Rebellion is largely reactive, a list of grievances against the Emperor and his Empire. Albeit that these grievances contain the seeds of freedom and democracy, there is no apparent plan to bring greater justice to the galaxy. Is this why the Rebellion seems to lack popular support?[1]

The Alliance's mission was to restore hope against an Empire that wants to crush dreams. Important though this is, our rebellion requires more. We need to tell a story about the corruption and crimes of empire, but not just seek to restore what has been lost. We need to stand for freedom, but spell out what real freedom is. We need to demand democracy, but recognize that in an open, pluralist, popular rebellion, leaders can come from anywhere. And we need to fight the battles right in front of us, but in ways that begin to build the new republic we want.

"The Belonging You Seek Is Not Behind You…It Is Ahead"

Even if we wanted to, we can't return to the republic we've lost. In contrast to 1990s' talk of a coming "progressive century," the decade since the global financial crisis has all but destroyed so-called centrism. Center-left parties have suffered defeats in almost all Western democracies.

Forced to choose sides by the crisis, the center-left struggled to tell a new story. Like the Jedi in the Separatist crisis, center-left parties were seen by many voters as part of the self-interested elites who caused the crash. Right-wing authoritarian populists gladly seized their chance, with simple stories about immigration, jobs, elite corruption, the iniquities of globalization and the loss of control to phantom menaces such as the European Union or the United Nations.

The center-left was so vulnerable because it had embraced a technocratic liberalism which largely accepted the assumptions of the new right's empire of markets. They said, we can manage the system, but in a fairer way. They didn't seem to care much about the dark forces that were on the move: widening inequality, the increasing power of the hyper-rich and the fracturing of republics into winners and losers from globalization.

They could have taken radical action. As Mike Lux among others argues, US Democrats (the same goes for many Western center-left parties) could have introduced fundamental reforms that would have recognized the anger of working-class voters at the way Wall Street had destroyed Main Street.[2] Had they fundamentally restructured the financial sector, immigration, energy policy, the criminal justice system and campaign finance, Democrats could have built a sustained governing majority similar to the one the New Deal had created in the 1930s. When they didn't, Democrats broke their own coalition.

The exceptions of the new left parties – most prominently Syriza in Greece, and Podemos in Spain – have brought new energy, ideas and ways of organizing to the left, but have faced massive opposition and not been able to lead the rebuilding of the left across Europe and beyond. Only more recently have Democrats and others seemingly learned the lesson: there is no movement in modest reforms to systems that many voters regard as fundamentally broken. As Kate Aronoff puts it: "Reconstituting the New Republic – the Obama era, in our case –

can only stave off the Sith for so long before recreating the same flaws that let the Empire take power the first time around. The Rebellion needs to be reborn nearly wholesale to win anything but pyrrhic victories."[3]

"Give Yourself to the Dark Side. It Is the Only Way You Can Save Your Friends"

In the *Star Wars* prequels, Palpatine's manipulation of the Clone Wars and purge of the Jedi handed him a fractured galaxy desperate for peace and stability. Order and justice are especially seductive messages because of the insecurity and injustice created by capitalism. And so we need to direct our attention to the root causes of Trumpism et al.

The decade after the crash brought to the fore trends which had been building for some time; deindustrialization, outsourcing, growing inequality and insecurity, the decline of working-class communities and the corruption of political systems. Any enduring solution to the problem that authoritarians represent needs to involve a comprehension of these forces.

For this, we need to foster a Jedi mindset unclouded by feelings such as rage and hatred that can lead to tactical blunders that end up helping Trump and his fellow authoritarians (at the same time, as we've seen, too much Jedi detachment is a bad thing). The temptation to dismiss Trump supporters as racists or fascists is simplistic and counterproductive. We need to understand what created those leanings so that we can root out the causes. This is critical to the struggle against empire. It's what it means to be radical.

"For the First Time I Have Something to Fight For"

On April 17, 1965, 25,000 people participated in a march on Washington DC organized by Students for a Democratic Society to end the war in Vietnam. After several hours of picketing the White House, the President of SDS, Paul Potter, spoke to demonstrators in front of the Washington Monument. His remarks became known as the "Incredible War" speech (or the "Naming the System" speech).[4] Rather than focusing on powerful "evil" individuals, Potter asked what kind of system is it that justifies war and colonialism, disenfranchisement and racial poverty, and still persists in calling itself "free"?[5]

In describing how we might overturn this system, Potter called for: "a movement based on the integrity of man and on a belief in man's capacity to determine his own life; ...a movement that has the capacity to tolerate all the formulations of society that men may choose to strive for..."

Our rebellion is for freedom. Indeed, freedom has always been what radical democratic left politics has been about – from fighting against segregation and for women's suffrage, to workplace representation, the minimum wage, social security and healthcare. These struggles have also been battles about the definition of freedom and who is granted it.

Left economic policy is essential to creating the conditions in which individuals can gain agency over their own lives.[6] The right's ideological revolution of the 1970s promised that deregulation, privatization and tax cuts for the rich would increase freedom and check private and public (government) power. But corporate power has grown substantially, as has the power of the state to threaten individual liberties. Now, the left needs to take freedom further, taking on concentrations of power such as monopolistic companies that seek to dominate the economy, degrade the environment and weaken the power of consumers, workers, voters and communities.[7]

The ultimate freedom is the freedom to choose political alternatives, which empire has sought to deny. As Chantal Mouffe argues, the central conflict in Western societies is between a right (authoritarian) and left (democratic) populism.[8] For this, we need to tell a story about a deeper democracy. A left-populist strategy should bring together struggles against subordination, oppression and discrimination, and reclaim the idea of "the people versus elites" from the authoritarian nationalist right.

As we'll see, this focus on freedom is resisted by parts of the left who see it as a capitulation to "bourgeois ideology." But as Albert Camus lamented, "The great event of the twentieth century was the forsaking of the values of freedom by the revolutionary movements. Since that moment a certain hope has disappeared from the world and a solitude has begun for each and every man."[9]

We also need to call out the false freedom offered by corporate-aligned, sometimes corporate-funded, so-called libertarians who equate "liberty" with dismantling and privatizing social security, all the while they ignore the crony capitalism of corporate welfare, military and prison spending. Genuine libertarians should be on our side, against both corporate and state authoritarianism. These are the real battle lines of our civil war: empire versus rebels.

"This Is a Rebellion, Isn't It? I Rebel"

To build a rebel alliance, the left needs to be expansionary and welcoming, continually extending rights and recognizing new voices. This isn't a distraction from the rebellion, it *is* the rebellion.

Solo, mostly reviewed as fan service entertainment, depicted how "new" voices for social justice are often ignored and marginalized. We are introduced to a radical droid, L3-37, Lando's co-pilot. She is conscious, autonomous and self-built (self-actualized, you might say). "Do you need anything?" Lando asks her. "Equal rights," L3-37 replies.

Echoing the film's liberation versus slavery theme, when L3-37 sees two droids being forced to cage fight for the entertainment of a baying crowd, she urges them to demand their freedom. She's told to mind her own business by the fight promoter. When she's tasked with creating a distraction at a mining facility on the planet Kessel, she releases the slaves and instigates a revolt. In the ensuing melee, she is struck down and dies.

This seemed to some critics like punishment for L3-37's "militancy." She becomes the very thing she fought against, a silent slave, by being uploaded into the Millennium Falcon. Alternatively, you can read L3-37's story as depicting what it takes to challenge the status quo. Rebellion can extract a price, but that's what fighting for justice means.

So-called radicalism has been how we have made progress, expanding freedom and rights to more people. As Robert Kuttner, a liberal centrist, has acknowledged, it wasn't liberals (let alone conservatives) who created what was most good in the republic, radicals did.[10] Nearly every great social justice movement was initiated by radicals before it became safe for liberals. Yesterday's rebels created what we want to save. Tomorrow's rebels will create a new republic.

"What If the Democracy We Thought We Were Serving No Longer Exists, and the Republic Has Become the Very Evil We've Been Fighting to Destroy?"

The United States is a corrupt oligarchy, its institutions manipulated by the hidden forces of dark money controlled by the billionaires of the radical right.[11] How long should we hang onto a democracy that may have already perished?

In the *Star Wars* films, this dilemma is exemplified by Padmé (Queen Amidala). She desperately tries to keep peace, avoid war and stop the galaxy dividing, not realizing that a greater disaster is already in motion. Following the invasion of Naboo, Padmé's frustration with the bureaucracy and corruption of the Republic leads to her calling a vote of no confidence in Chancellor Valorum, opening the way for Palpatine's plan for Empire.[12] She's wise to abhor war but naive to fail to see its inevitability.[13] Even in *Attack of the Clones*, when Queen Jamillia insists that, "We must keep our faith in the Republic. The day we stop believing democracy can work is the day we lose it," Padmé agrees. Her idealism dooms her and the Republic.[14]

Such is the vulnerability of already weakened republics to (real and fabricated) crises. We can't afford to be naive about the intentions of those who are driven to accumulate power and wealth. *Star Wars* dramatizes the false choice between flawed democracy and fascist dictatorship. The better choice is made by Princess Leia, who recognizes the evil of the Empire but stays in the Senate to the end, secretly helping to lead the Rebellion. We need to rebel against the republic in order to save it.

"If You Will Not Fight, Then You Will Meet Your Destiny"

For the best of reasons, liberals resist the idea of enemies and hope that democratic deliberation can produce acceptable compromises. But what about when there are real enemies of people and planet, of democracy and freedom? As Becky Sharp (albeit writing from a different political perspective) notes:

> Evil in Star Wars is like a cancer; it has to be utterly defeated or else all is lost. Over and over through the six films, compromise with evil is shown to be a mistake even if there is good intent behind it. Luke refuses to compromise himself, even to the point of sacrificing his life...Obi-Wan's "only a Sith deals in absolutes" is perplexing or at least ironic because the saga itself has absolutes throughout.[15]

As Robert Kuttner recognizes, "radicals are more likely to appreciate the political dynamics of capitalism as an obstacle to the reforms that liberals would like to carry out...So if the terms of global capitalism are finally becoming debatable, we can thank the young radicals for forcing the issue."[16] What we can see more clearly than ever is that no policies can serve the people and the powerful at once, especially when it comes to averting climate chaos. There is no third way between civilization and collapse. As in all civil wars, we need to choose a side.

"If We Do Not Act Quickly, All Will Be Lost Forever"

While we need to look forward, part of our story involves looking back. Not to some utopia that never existed, but to remind us what is possible and what the new right has taken away.

The myth of the right is that white, male, middle-aged power is essential to security and order. But that power is slipping away, even as it seems at its most dominant (hence all their squealing).

The conservative story of the past is a fiction. They want to go back to the 1950s, but not to the social programs, infrastructure investment, cheap college, not-for-profit healthcare, strong banking regulations or higher taxes on the rich that helped to build the American middle class and the strongest economy in the world. We need to promote the alternative myth, the meaningful popular belief, of a society that was built in the interests of ordinary people, even if, like the Galactic Republic, that freedom and democracy was far from realized.

The influence of mythologist Joseph Campbell on *Star Wars* has been overstated, but his codification of world myths contains some useful insights for our story. Campbell divided his monomyth into three main stages – Departure, Initiation and Return. Rebels are forced to "leave home" to restore balance to the world. In Campbell's terms, destroying the Death Star is the "world-restoring task." But this doesn't allow the hero to return to the past, since it doesn't exist anymore. The world is renewed, but it has also changed irrevocably. Saving what we love means accepting that a new world will be born.

For example, in *Climate, A New Story*, Charles Eisenstein proposes a change in the story used by the climate movement.[17] Rather than focusing on rising carbon emissions or the economic value of ecosystems, Eisenstein suggests that environmentalists tell a much more emotional story about a love of nature, about protection and loss. Instead of impending catastrophe, we need to cultivate meaningful emotional and psychological connections which form the foundation for real, actionable steps to care for the planet.

The dark side longs for a past in which power was held by a few. The light side really is love – love for what was good in the past, for what can be saved, but also for what could be to come.

"Congratulations. You Are Being Rescued. Please Do Not Resist"

But who tells these stories? Should our rebellion be led by a so-called revolutionary vanguard?

Of course, any rebellion needs its leaders and thinkers. But we can't build a better democracy by behaving anti-democratically. Our story won't work if it is just about a small group of leaders, neither will the new republic we want to build.

Star Wars plays out these tensions. In general, the Rebels seem more vanguardist. We mostly only see a small Rebel Alliance. Then again, *The Last Jedi*'s anti-elitist theme and its democratizing of the Force suggest that rebellions against overwhelmingly more powerful forces can't depend on the heroics of the few. Yet at the end of the film, the depleted Resistance calls for help from the rest of the galaxy and their call is ignored. Perhaps the Rebels are paying the price for their failure to build popular support.

As we'll discuss in the next episode, our assumptions about radical leadership are changing. The new awakening of protest groups and campaigners reject hierarchy in how they organize and in the world they want to see. This reflects a broader shift reflected in popular culture. Jeff Gomez, a writer and transmedia producer in fantasy, science fiction and young adult genres, has written about how we are shifting from the hero's journey to a collective journey, to ensemble-based narratives with multiple protagonists, missions and ways of succeeding.[18]

In our deliberately depoliticizing society, many people

find politics boring and divisive. But a collective journey story offers far more potential for engaging them. Collective stories (Gomez uses *The Last Jedi* as an example) tell us that headstrong masculinity is over; contrast this with the right's savior worship and some of the twentieth century's most destructive stories. Our new stories are about communities, intersectional coalitions for action, struggling to achieve systemic change through the power of their differences but drawn together by universal values. Together, we must become our own salvation.

"Chewie, We're Home"

In his 1973 book *The Image of the Future*, Dutch historian and sociologist Fred Polak argued that we've entered a "timeless time" because of the "de-utopianising of utopia."[19] To Polak, we are inherently future-creating beings, citizens of two worlds, the present and the imagined. But writing a few years before *A New Hope*, Polak thought that visions of the future had become nihilistic and full of despair. A generation of young people desperately need to know it is possible to create better futures. Without this, we live in a broken culture.

However true, Ernst Bloch (we said we'd return to him) argued that the process of reaching utopia is a self-generating one. At its best, the utopian tendency (as experienced in popular stories, among other places) helps us to understand the heroic element in history and provide glimpses of possible futures.

Like Marx, Bloch rejected utopian communism. Instead, we are in an inevitable process propelled by creating and producing human beings driven by their material needs and their dreams of overcoming these needs. The society we end up with will be the product of the process of getting there, and the process is made by those who are made by the process.

In episode I, we made the point that *Star Wars* is about choice, about taking action in the absence of grand plans. There's nothing leftist in denying the agency of ordinary people to decide their own fate, or of the possibility contained in everyday actions. If we forget about utopia and pay attention to the day-to-day business of challenging the empire that exists all around us, we might stand a better chance of bringing into being the radical social transformation we want. As Wes Bishop suggests, reflecting on *Rogue One* and the political ethics of *Star Wars*:

> The state of hope is founded on a belief that real change can occur. Therefore hope, true hope, is grounded in practicality. It understands historic limitations, but more importantly it understands history. It grounds itself in the knowledge that what currently exists will not, cannot, always exist...In this way hope inspires direct action. It is where we build our rebellions, our movements, our conscious calls for change. It is where we become historic actors moving through time, not as fabled legendary heroes, but as flawed, contradictory beings.[20]

To Bloch, one day we will reach a place we have never been before but it will feel like home.

"This Bickering Is Pointless"
The lack of a single utopia opens up the possibility of a more pluralist left. But this doesn't mean a lack of broader unity. As Charles Derber suggests in *Welcome to the Revolution*, only a new universalizing wave, a progressive and revolutionary movement of movements, can counter the world-universalizing forces of intensifying corporate and hard-right power.[21]

Again, we can look back to the 1960s new left for inspiration. Revolutionary moments like 1968 see the large-scale mobilization of many different sectors of society. New groups come to the fore, highlighting different issues and forms of struggle. As Laurence Cox suggests:

[O]ne of the tasks of revolutionaries in the present is to engage with this reality. This runs counter to most forms of sectarian learning, as it does to other forces shaping much of the radical left: the niche markets of intellectual commodities within which people come to identify and consume as anarchists, feminists, Marxists, autonomists, anti-racists and so on; and the equally specialized structures of radical academia...Revolutionary praxis involves learning to listen to these new voices, without automatically comparing them to the sets of ideas we have invested in and finding them – inevitably – wanting...[22]

It's about finding shared points of alliance, including between those who want to tweak the existing order and those who want to challenge its larger structures of power. This means abandoning the idea that one tradition of progressive thought has all the answers.[23] The best way to resist the lure of fascism is to live its opposite. Why would we want to replace one empire with another? As Denis Wood emphasizes, at the end of *A New Hope* we are left with an indeterminacy, necessarily so:

Not only is Luke the character who most personally confronts the effects of fascism, but he is pulled between the poles of its alternatives, anarchism in the person of Han and representative democracy in the person of Leia. In the end, he does not choose and so remains free of dogma, not ripped in two, but whole and together...[I]f the film is determinedly anti-fascist it offers no pat alternatives: there is no simple way to steer clear of the fascist mesh.[24]

"Now You Will Pay the Price for Your Lack of Vision"
There seem to be two main views of the strategy and organization of the Rebel Alliance in *Star Wars*: highly disciplined, or hopelessly lacking in direction.

The Rebels are a military resistance movement, headed by the Alliance High Command. Prior to its official founding, various rebel cells operated their own military forces. But they presented little threat to the Emperor as long as they remained isolated and uncoordinated, so a galaxy-wide revolutionary intergalactic movement was formed. Although individual groups maintained their existing structures and had some autonomy in their regions, strategic command of the Alliance became the responsibility of leaders such as Mon Mothma. The Advisory Council, the political leadership of the Rebellion, was composed of representatives from the seven planets whose populations had the highest casualties inflicted by the Empire.

To some military and strategic commentators, the Alliance repeatedly reveals its lack of discipline. For the blogger Angry Staff Officer for example, *The Last Jedi* demonstrates how the Resistance lacks great generals.[25] Poe Dameron gambles on a shot to take out a First Order star destroyer in violation of a direct order from Leia. The mission succeeds in knocking out the ship but at the cost of the Resistance bomber fleet. (Then again, in *Rogue One* the plans for the Death Star would not have been stolen were it not for a small band of rebels betraying orders.)

Rather than making massive sacrifices for little gain, the strength of the Resistance rests in its ability to survive. It shares this trait with real-world rebellions throughout history. Most get worn down through attrition and a lack of resources; a decisive battle becomes a tempting way to make a grand statement but often proves to be a mistake. By refusing to learn the rules of unity of command and the necessity of preserving their forces, the Resistance brings itself to the brink.

We've already rejected vanguardism. But where is strategy and coordination supposed to come from in a diverse and democratic rebellion? One interesting view has been put forward by Michael Hardt and Antonio Negri in their series of books (*Empire*, *Multitude*, *Commonwealth* and *Assembly*). As we'll discuss in the next episode, in recent years seemingly leaderless social movements have proliferated around the globe, from North Africa and the Middle East to Europe, the Americas and East Asia. But with the rise of hard right-wing parties and movements in many countries, the question of how to organize both democratically and effectively has become urgent. On their own, today's leaderless political organizations may not be sufficient, but a return to traditional, centralized forms of political leadership is neither desirable nor possible.

Instead, as Hardt and Negri argue, familiar roles should be reversed: leaders are responsible for short-term, tactical action, but it is the multitude who must drive strategy. New social movements must invent effective modes of assembly and decision-making structures that rely on the broadest democratic base to take power differently. In this way, we might avoid Poe Dameron-like errors but also build the wider popular support that the rebel alliance needs.

"Attacking That Battle Station Is Not My Idea of Courage. It's More Like, Suicide"

As economists sometimes do, presumably as a break from more boring things, in 2015 Zachary Feinstein, a professor at Washington University in St Louis, published a study on the impact of destroying the Death Stars.[26] His finding: the Empire was too big to fail.

In the OT, two Death Stars got blown up and then the government fell, all within 4 years. Feinstein's paper attempts to measure the level of systemic risk this shockwave caused in the galaxy's banking and financial systems. He assumes that banks invested heavily in the Empire; somewhat typically for an economist, he doesn't stop to consider what it says politically that the financial sector was quite happy to fund space fascism.

In any case, Feinstein estimates that the fall of Empire means that the government would default on $515.5 quintillion in bonds, causing the financial system to collapse and requiring a rescue of more than 1700 banks: "[T]he Rebel Alliance would need to prepare a bailout of at least 15%, and likely at least 20%, of [Gross Galactic Product] in order to mitigate the systemic risks and the sudden and catastrophic economic collapse...Without such funds at the ready, it's likely the Galactic economy would enter an economic depression of astronomical proportions."[27]

This is how empire holds a (ray) gun to our heads. The system is so big it seems impossible to replace without catastrophic consequences. And yet, what choice do we have, when the system itself is leading to even bigger catastrophic consequences?

"This Is Some Rescue! You Came In Here and You Didn't Have a Plan for Getting Out?"

In spite of some leftists' pessimism, we can envisage a different society, a much better republic. Indeed, we already have much of the technological and intellectual knowledge we need to tackle the challenges we face; the problem is the system under which we live. What capitalist realism desperately tries to distract us from is that it's not really that difficult to envisage what a post-capitalist society could look like: a fundamental dismantling of corporate monopoly power; much more decentralized and localized economies with democratic public planning; less commodification of every damn thing in our lives; more common resources held in community trust; less wage labor; more self-management of our work and creative endeavors; radically less precarious lives; much more universal provision of our basic needs. Cooperatives and associations of small businesses, farmers, workers, credit unions, mutual banks, mutual aid societies...Local renewable energy generation and food production. Green community factories. Automation and artificial intelligence made to work for people rather than being weaponized against them. User-designed and delivered public services, social care systems and healthcare providers...

Such is the intellectual totalitarianism of empire that many people think that such forms of cooperation and collaboration are impossible. Anakin, quoting his mother, says, "the biggest problem in this universe is nobody helps each other." But it isn't true. We are not the selfish individualists that empire needs us to believe we are. As Rebecca Solnit puts it:

"[H]ow powerful are the altruistic, idealistic forces already at work in the world. ...[V]ast amounts of how we live our everyday lives – our interactions with and commitments to family lives, friendships, avocations, membership in social, spiritual and political organizations – are in essence noncapitalist or even anticapitalist, made up of things we do for free, out of love and on principle...Activists often speak as though the solutions we need have not yet been launched or invented, as though we are starting from scratch, when often the real goal is to amplify the power and reach of existing options. What we dream of is already present in the world."[28]

"Noooooooo!"

You know what would really interest me to do? Don't denounce me as a Stalinist but...Star Wars presenting Palpatine and Darth Vader as good, progressive, egalitarian centralists fighting reactionary, feudalist all those Jedi bullshit particulars, to tell totally the opposite story from the other's point [of view]. What do they stand for, all that Republic blah blah..? No![29]

Slavoj Žižek's characteristically humorous-but-maybe-actually-serious remarks suggest the lurking menace of a left empirism.[30] As Yoda once said, "Revealed, your opinion is."

Today's communist revivalists such as Žižek and Jodi Dean regard democracy as so tainted by neoliberalism and so meaningless that it distracts from the struggle against capitalism.[31] But surely the fact that new right authoritarians continuously seek to erode democracy tells us that they still fear its potential, and that the struggle against the inequities of capitalism and for democracy is the same thing. As Nicos Poulantzas wrote in *State, Power, Socialism* in 1978, "socialism will be democratic, or it will not be at all."[32]

As we'll see in the next episode, anti-capitalist rebellions are everywhere bubbling below the surface, and increasingly above it. The real impulse of anti-capitalist resistance is coming from the anarchist, autonomist and anti-authoritarian left. The communist revivalists suggest that these movements represent revolt without revolution and criticize brave rebels as obstacles to a "proper confrontation" with the ongoing crisis of our economic system. Instead, they argue that we should wait patiently for the Big Future Event, the cataclysmic act of upheaval that will give birth to a glorious new world.[33] As K-2SO would say, "I find that answer vague and unconvincing."

The truth is, we don't need a "left alternative to democracy." We just need democracy, and the struggle for it is going on all around us.

And here's a pertinent warning from *Star Wars* history. As described in the 2016 novel *Star Wars: Bloodline* by Claudia Gray, a few years before the events of *The Force Awakens* the New Republic's Senate divided into two parties: the Populists led by Leia, who want to decentralize authority; and the Centrists, who want to concentrate power in a strong central government. Some of the Centrists are former Imperials who admire the Empire for bringing order to the galaxy, and who fear that without strong central control the New Republic will become as ineffectual as the Galactic Republic. Ultimately, many Centrist worlds secede from the New Republic to reunite with Imperial remnants on the fringe of the galaxy and combine into a new government called, yes, the First Order. Most of those in the Senate are happy to see the Centrists go, judging that the First Order controls far too little of the galaxy to pose any threat…

"There Are Alternatives to Fighting"

To the famous scene in Kevin Smith's *Clerks*, in which a character questions the Rebel Alliance's attack on the second Death Star:

> A construction job of that magnitude would require a helluva lot more manpower than the Imperial army had to offer. I'll bet there were independent contractors working on that thing: plumbers, aluminum siders, roofers…All of a sudden these left-wing militants blast you with lasers and wipe out everyone within a three-mile radius. You didn't ask for that. You have no personal politics. You're just trying to scrape out a living.[34]

Some revolutionaries' apparent longing for a violent transformation of society recalls the Emperor's attempt at manipulating Luke at the end of *Return of the Jedi*: "Now, release your anger. Only your hatred can destroy me."[35] More often, the opposite is true.

Many campaigners and activists have long argued that nonviolence is more effective than violence.[36] Others suggest there are no easy maxims and that in some situations a mixed approach may cause less suffering than a strict adherence to nonviolence.[37]

Even if true, fascists love violence, and authorities will seek (and often invent) any justification to quash resistance. Instead, Mahatma Gandhi spoke of *satyagraha* as the basis for his strategic campaigns of nonviolent civil resistance – the truth force, or the power of holding on to truth. Nonviolence, or *ahimsa*, is less an idea than a physical reality, a force at once physical and moral, pervading the universe. It's not really about peaceful protest, it's about mastering your will, individually and collectively, and transforming the terms of the debate. It's about making the situation as uncomfortable for oppressors.

If this sounds rather Jedi-like, that's no coincidence. George Lucas was clearly influenced by Eastern philosophies in developing the idea of the Force (called the Force of Others in early drafts of *A New Hope*): the dualities of light and dark, love and fear, and avoiding extremes and urging moderation in all things.[38] And as dramatized in the films, while the energy of anger can drive us to act, it is hope and humanity that sustains rebellion and leads to victory.

While *Star Wars* is sometimes accused of glorifying violence as a means of political action, key moments in the films revolve around the wisdom of avoiding it. In *Return of the Jedi*'s final confrontation, Luke discards his weapon rather than strike down Darth Vader and succumb to the dark side (this is echoed in the climax to *The Last Jedi*, when Luke "confronts" Kylo Ren in order to save his friends). Risking death, Luke rejects the lure of violence and domination, and so his father's generational values – a truly revolutionary act.[39] As Mark Eldridge surmises:

Fighting when you have no other choice, to stand in defense of others, is Good; fighting from a place of anger or hatred is Bad. The ethics of Star Wars are not consequentialist – it has a strong value system and motivations are as important as results. Fighting with anger – tapping into the dark side – may yield quick, positive results, but it will come at a great cost, which will ultimately be your soul.[40]

"What Mission? What Are You Talking About?"

In 2003, Arundhati Roy wrote that:

Our strategy should be not only to confront empire, but to lay siege to it. To deprive it of oxygen. To shame it. To mock it. With our art, our music, our literature, our stubbornness, our joy, our brilliance, our sheer relentlessness – and our ability to tell our own stories. Stories that are different from the ones we're being brainwashed to believe.[41]

In *Star Wars*, George Lucas found a way to tell an accessible and popular story of rebellion through approachable characters, simple dynamics, historical allusions, humor, a palpable sense of crisis and a profound belief in choice. But what is our story of rebellion?

It is a period of civil war. The REPUBLIC had lasted for decades. But it was an imperfect order, plagued by inequality and exclusion. An alliance of new left REBELS challenges the republic. They want to make the republic's values real for all its citizens.

Fearing anarchy, EMPIRE strikes back. From a network of think tanks hidden around the planet, the sinister NEW RIGHT draws up secret plans to resurrect the power of CAPITAL and crush the growing rebellion. Pursued by imperial agents in the media, big business, and finance, the rebels splinter and flee.

EMPIRE reigns. Step-by-step, policies dismantle the republic and impose the unquestionable forces of the market. Empire expands to the furthest reaches of the planet. Everyone is subject to its new order. Empire promises peace and security but relies on domination and fear.

Soon, TURMOIL engulfs empire. An unsustainable death star economy spreads its shadow across the planet, riddled with corporate corruption, monopoly power, inequality and exploitation. People's hopelessness turns to anger, seized on by a new order of EMPERORS who plot to introduce tyranny.

But there has been a new awakening. Igniting a spark of hope, RESISTANCE is forming. People are fighting back against the exploitative, crisis-ridden, planet-destroying empire. Only a REBEL ALLIANCE can save democracy and build a NEW REPUBLIC to restore freedom and justice.

Empire fears that millions of people could join the rebellion and imperial control over the galaxy will be lost forever. But there isn't much time. If the rebels are too late, we will lose everything...

Episode VI

"There Has Been an Awakening. Have You Felt It?"

"It's True. The Force, the Jedi, All of It. It's All True"

There would be no rebels without empire, but equally there might not be empire without rebels.

In *Star Wars*, the Delegation of 2000 decrying Chancellor Palpatine's constitutional changes represented the start of the Rebellion; the Emperor issued arrest warrants for the majority of those who had signed its declaration. Bail Organa and Mon Mothma maintained an outward appearance of obedience, but behind the scenes they masterminded the unification of various insurgents into the Rebel Alliance.[1] Of course, those who wish for a fairer, more equal world aren't responsible for the oppression of empire. Rather, empire is threatened by our resistance.[2]

We've already mentioned Michael Hardt and Antonio Negri's book *Empire*. The neoliberalism of the 1980s was a revolution from above, a response to the potential revolution from below of industrial action and the new left we noted in episodes II and III. This is how, as Hardt and Negri put it, the multitude called empire into being.

Empire is now creating another rebellion. This episode focuses on young people, activism and campaigning. Beyond these activists, the majority of young people aren't on the side of empire. To paraphrase Princess Leia, the more that empire tightens its grip, the more young people slip through its fingers. But they still need to be brought into our rebellion, one that grows and progressively pushes back on the power of empire to exploit and oppress.

"The Empire's Time Has Come. You Don't Have to Go Down with It"

Empire controls the economic system, financial institutions, governments, the most powerful media. It has police forces and armies, courts and prisons. If empire has this much power, what chance do we have? And yet...

Reflecting on the spin-off story *Solo*, Amy Erica Smith points out the Empire's territorial control is so spotty that arguably it cannot claim to be a state in the modern sense at all.[3] Strong states maintain control through co-option, not repression. They socialize citizens to regard their rule as legitimate, partly by providing public goods, from economic growth to justice systems. In this respect, the more successful a regime, the less it has to use its formal power or its brute force against its citizens/subjects. In contrast, states that rely on brutality for compliance tend to be weak and based around a particular leader; they often have a fairly short life.

In *Star Wars*, the Empire relies on force. Its stormtroopers constantly patrol occupied territories, always scanning for rebel threats, while its Star Destroyers hover menacingly above. Not that it would make for a particularly dramatic scene, but no-one is ever shown equivocating about Imperial rule ("on the one hand..."). Only its armies parrot its propaganda.[4] Such is the lack of love for Empire it even has to blow up planets to induce "respect." Of course, it would have been better to provide the galaxy's citizens with at least the basic public goods that help to legitimize states, the real security that comes from welfare, employment, health and social care etc. But as we know, all of its efforts to induce fear are ultimately ineffective; it fuels the resistance that will eventually destroy it.

Given the Empire's fundamental weaknesses, it's no surprise that Palpatine's dictatorship only lasts for 22 years, less than a human generation (the Republic lasted for a thousand years). Empires that provide people with little hope and little hope for change are doomed. Our empire has its own weaknesses. Like the Empire, it might seem all-encompassing. But its exceptional claim to universalism, that there is no alternative, is its greatest vulnerability. If this is the only system there is, we demand that it should be better, fairer, more just. And when it can't be, because it is fundamentally unjust and exploitative, when it embraces authoritarianism in response to rising public anger, it gives too many people little hope and little hope for change...

"Evacuate!?! In Our Moment of Triumph?"

Another problem with empires is that they increasingly believe their own propaganda, all the while their subjects increasingly don't. As Luke said to the Emperor, "Your overconfidence is your weakness." Rather than mocking and deriding resistance, empire should be asking why it is growing. As in *Star Wars*, there is little love for our empire. Indeed, capitalist realism effectively acknowledges this. It says, we know you don't like it, but this is all there is. And yet, more and more people are recognizing that this is *not* all there is.

Rebellion is proliferating. Trump and his fellow authoritarians are creating new political activists, ordinary people who for the first time find themselves protesting, participating, organizing, running for office, making connections This has been happening for some time. Naturally, it ebbs and flows – from the new left of the 1960s to the alternative economic thinking of the 1970s and 1980s, from the "anti-globalization" movement and protests of the late 1990s, the anti-war campaigns of the early 2000s, to the real democracy movements of the 2010s including Occupy and the Arab Spring.

As we'll see, critics question whether these waves of often autonomous, leaderless forms of grassroots resistance can mount a real opposition to empire. What is certain, however, is that they are not going away; they continue to adapt and develop and spread, testing and identifying weaknesses in the battle armor of empire and seizing new opportunities. And like the Rebel factions in *Star Wars*, they will find a way to come together.

As Mark Fisher argued, capitalist realism was only ever a fantasy, that the human resources capital needs for its growth are as infinite as its own appetites. Capital is now coming up on limits of all kinds, and for all the posturing of its agents, empire's propaganda isn't cutting it. The real enemy which prompted the neoliberal counter-revolution is re-emerging. It was never Stalinist communism, rather it was the various strains of democratic socialism and libertarian communism that burst through in so many places during the 1960s and 1970s.

The (truth) force is with us, and it is awakening. As Jennifer Gidley, a former President of the World Futures Studies Federation, has reflected: "In spite of the potential for catastrophe that current trends suggest, we are also in the best position ever to turn negative trends around through the means at our disposal. As a species, we have never been more conscious, more globally connected, or more capable of radical positive change than we are today."[5]

The Death Star is hubris in Quadanium steel plates. The Empire is not indestructible. Indeed, its design as a fear machine belies the Empire's terror of non-empire – of freedom, autonomy, of real choice and alternatives. We are starting to outnumber them, or rather, we are realizing that we always have. Rebel agents are everywhere; we have infiltrated imperial ranks, we are inside empire's chilly conference rooms, we play along with its rigid bureaucratic systems – but we dream of bringing its hollow Death Star down.

"I Don't Like It. I Don't Agree with It. But I Accept It"

Awakening is about taking responsibility, a key theme in *Star Wars*. Luke moves from "I can't get involved" hopelessness to a heroic maturity. Han *Solo* moves from "I'm only in it for the money" cynicism to helping his comrades. All of the main characters in *A New Hope* make a journey from resignation to rebellion: princess to rebel leader, farm boy to fighter pilot, smuggler to freedom fighter, aged hermit to militant martyr. The necessity of resistance and the slim possibility of victory bring them to life; it *is* life. But crucially, the journey that mythologist Joseph Campbell's archetypal hero undertakes is not an individualistic one, it's to aid her community: "[T]he ultimate aim of the quest must be neither release nor ecstasy for oneself, but the wisdom and the power to serve others."[6]

We are all part of empire, but we can all embark on a hero's journey. And here is where we need to diverge from fantasy and science fiction, since history teaches us that defeating the system is not just about throwing one Emperor off a balcony into a canyon of steel (to be fair, in *Star Wars* Darth Sidious's "death" doesn't end empirism either). Rather, as Mark Fisher stated:

> To reclaim a real political agency means first of all accepting our insertion at the level of desire in the remorseless meat-grinder of Capital. What is being disavowed in the abjection of evil and ignorance onto fantasmatic Others is our own complicity in planetary networks of oppression. What needs to be kept in mind is both that capitalism is a hyper-abstract impersonal structure and that it would be nothing without our co-operation.[7]

You might think that "empire" as a way of describing our system is overdoing it. Sure, it's not perfect, but it's not totalitarianism, right? In many countries, we still have rights and freedoms, we can criticize the government, we can read (and write) books like this…All of that is true and important. But as we've discussed, in all sorts of philosophical, intellectual, emotional and practical ways, perhaps in the future we might look back and recognize that:

We learned not to believe in anything, to ignore one another, to care only about ourselves...The previous regime – armed with its arrogant and intolerant ideology – reduced man to a force of production, and nature to a tool of production...of some monstrously huge, noisy and stinking machine, whose real meaning was not clear to anyone. We had all become used to the...system and accepted it as an unchangeable fact and thus helped to perpetuate it...None of us is just its victim. We are all also its co-creators.[8]

This was said by the former dissident Czech writer Václav Havel (later elected his country's president) about the contaminated moral environment of life under communist totalitarianism.

"I Must Obey My Master"

Empire is powerful. It has numerous ways of keeping us in line or buying us off.

Joseph Campbell was no radical and seemed to believe that the system couldn't be changed. Nonetheless, he recognized what happens when you conform: "[Y]ou get this Vader...He isn't thinking, or living in terms of humanity, he's living in terms of a system."[9]

As Wes Bishop points out, the dark side is so dangerous because it *doesn't* advertise its evil.[10] Rather, it wriggles its way into our thinking, latching onto our desires, corrupting us from inside. It's the moral relativism of Sith thinking that makes this corruption possible; if the light and dark side are two sides to the same coin, why not embrace the dark side? Especially when it promises a path to what we desire, and what we desire seems perfectly justifiable, moral even. All that Jedi stuff is just holding us back.

But as Han Solo once said in a different context, "No reward is worth this." Not to become like Vader, our humanity consumed. Following orders, even when we know they're wrong? As Jyn

Erso retorts in *Rogue One*, "You may as well be a stormtrooper."

The answer, the radical solution, is not just to check our desires, but to work to create a system that is human in its design, that we can be truly moral within. As the activist Chris Crass writes:

> At the heart of the transformative justice commitment in the Alliance...is a historical and structural analysis of the Empire and how its evil forces people into compromise...into both inflicting suffering on others and feeling powerless to end one's own suffering. The Alliance has clarity about the impact of the Empire not only on the Galaxy, but on the hearts and minds of everyday people. Alongside...is a profound love and belief in everyday people to be authors of their own destiny and to make the universe more just and equitable in the process...[T]he Alliance understands that this is a fight for all of their lives, for their children, for their future.[11]

Since as George Lucas said, "The main theme for the overall downfall of the Empire – it was basically overcome by humanity."[12]

"Someone Has to Save Our Skins"

In *The Last Jedi*, Kylo Ren tries to break Rey by saying, "You have no place in this story. You come from nothing. You're nothing." Empire wants us to believe this, but it's not true.

In *Star Wars*, the new hope lies in young people. Luke is described as being 18 years old in the script. Leia might be 19, but she's maybe the most important person in the galaxy. From the first time we meet her, she refuses to be intimidated by Darth Vader and the Empire's extensive apparatus of fear. Moreover, given their age, these young people had never known anything but the Empire, and yet they envisaged its overthrow.

The activist and organizer Andrew Slack has noted the

prevalence of "orphans versus empires" in much popular fantasy, from Dorothy in the *Wizard of Oz*, and Superman and many other superheroes, to Harry Potter.[13] There are a lot of orphans in *Star Wars* as well. For a start, all of the Jedi are orphans, taken away from their parents at an early age to learn the discipline of their order. Luke's surrogate parents are killed, and later his real father dies as well. Leia's surrogate father is killed on Alderaan. Han, Rey, Finn, Jyn, Cassian And or…all orphans in one way or another. Most of them end up working for a better galaxy. Only Anakin, Kylo Ren and Boba Fett convert their pain and loss into anger and hatred.

As Andrew suggests, this isn't a coincidence, no universal stories are. As we push further into the world, we discover our own orphanhood. We are all orphans of a system that has abandoned humanity.

We need to hope that James Martin was right about young people. Martin, who died in 2013, is regarded as one of the most influential people in the history of computer science. He predicted the impact of the internet in his Pulitzer Prize nominated book *The Wired Society* (1978). In 2006 he published *The Meaning of the 21st Century*, in which he predicts that the world will undergo a major, difficult and disruptive transition during the twenty-first century, as significant as the industrial revolution. But Martin believed that this transition could be the beginning of fundamentally new forms of progress which greatly enhance affluence and culture while healing the environment. This will give meaning to the lives of today's young people:

The Transition Generation will not sit around and watch their world being unnecessarily damaged. Their frustrated desires to remake the world and address problems that they have inherited from the 20th century need not result in social unrest…Today's youth are more informed and educated. They understand the complexity of 21st century problems, and they do not seek simplistic answers. Indeed, the challenge of these problems excites and animates them.[14]

As we'll see next, there are many ways in which young people are leading. Many of them were forced into doing so by experience. Painful though it might be, once we recognize our own orphanhood, we might recall what Cassian says to Jyn in *Rogue One*: "Some of us live this Rebellion. I've been in this fight since I was six years old. You're not the only one who lost everything. Some of us just decided to do something about it."

"Impressive. Most Impressive"

A whole series of books couldn't do justice to all of the individuals, groups, communities and campaigns that are rising up.[15] The new new left, the young left (does it matter whether we label them as "the left" or not?) aren't listening to the pessimism and passivity of some of their elders. Nor do they fall for the lies of empire. To paraphrase Emma González, one of the leaders of the #NeverAgain movement, this is a "no BS" generation of activists and campaigners.

For example, the indigenous groups who are standing up against the exploitation of their lands by extraction industries, most notably the Dakota Access Pipeline protests that began in early 2016 in reaction to the approved construction of the pipeline in the northern United States. The Standing Rock Sioux tribe ignited a new phase in the indigenous rights movement; hundreds of groups and nonindigenous allies gathered to resist the building of the pipeline. The message of Standing Rock spread across tribes, countries and continents – a complex and multilayered movement calling for environmental reform, indigenous sovereignty and human rights.

Or Black Lives Matter, which began in 2013 with a social media hashtag and has grown into a decentralized international activist movement that campaigns against violence and systemic racism. BLM protests against police killings of black people and broader issues such as racial profiling and racial inequality in the criminal justice system. Patrisse Cullors, one of its founders, described the movement's mission as "Provid[ing] hope and inspiration for collective action to build collective power to achieve collective transformation, rooted in grief and rage but pointed towards vision and dreams." BLM is inspired by the Black Power movement, 1980s Black feminism, Pan-Africanism, the Anti-Apartheid movement, hip hop, LGBTQ equality campaigns and Occupy. But its "group-centered model of leadership" differentiates it from the older charismatic leadership model of earlier civil rights organizations.[16]

Or what happened after Valentine's Day 2018, when shooting erupted at Marjory Stoneman Douglas high school in Parkland, Florida. Remarkably, heroically, the students almost immediately led an uprising against lax gun laws.[17] Just 5 weeks later they had organized the March for Our Lives, one of the largest protests in US history.[18] They have inspired millions of Americans to join a grassroots movement against corrupted politicians who stand against gun safety reforms and challenged a media that covers breaking mass murder but not the campaigns that could stop it happening. The Parkland students continue to march for change, through media campaigns, school walkouts, voter drives and calling politicians to account. With a moral force and clarity equivalent to the civil rights movement, this generation has made it clear that problems previously deemed unsolvable due to powerful lobbies and political cowardice are theirs to solve. As Emma González says, "This generation is revolutionary because we want to live."

So it is with another set of school walkouts. There have been climate change protests before.[19] But now, outside of pre-existing structures, young people are leading them. In August 2018, Greta Thunberg, a 15-year-old Swedish activist, refused to attend school so that she could protest outside her national parliament building. Ever since, school climate strikes have spread around the world. Tens and tens of thousands of students are regularly protesting. The Youth Strikes for Climate movement is not centrally organized, so keeping track of the fast-growing number of strikes is impossible, but hundreds of events took place on 15 March 2019 across more than 50 countries, making it the biggest strike day so far.[20]

As Mark and Paul Engler suggest in their *This Is an Uprising*, this type of "momentum-driven organizing" goes beyond transactional goals by advancing a transformational agenda.[21] It is attentive to the symbolic properties of campaigns, just as much as instrumental demands. It is willing to polarize public opinion and risk controversy with bold protests, but maintains nonviolent discipline so as not to undermine broad-based public support. And it is conscious of the need to work with other organizing traditions to institutionalize gains and foster alternative communities that can sustain resistance over the longer-term.

There are many ways to connect these diverse movements: as mass mobilizations against violence and oppression, in their recognition of the systemic nature of what we're up against and by their refusal to accept so-called pragmatism and political realities. They are also about freedom, not some abstract notion of "freedom" but real freedom – from the exploitation of land and environment, police brutality and institutional injustice, to being afraid at school and climate chaos. Just like our favorite fictional rebellion, they fight for the freedom necessary for survival.

"We Would Be Honored If You Would Join Us"

These movements are also changing the story, literally. As Doyle Canning and Patrick Reinsborough note, they are helping society to re-narrate the present political reality.[22] Environmental justice groups are exposing greed-driven fossil fuel companies and culpable public officials as villains. Police shootings of black men can no longer be dismissed as isolated incidents. "We are the 99 percent" helped make discussions of rampant inequality, even oligarchy, unavoidable. No longer are crushing college debts, medical bills or families facing foreclosure just seen as individual problems, but instead as public crises with systemic roots.

It's not just about being communications savvy. Growing up in a world saturated with media, "the kids" not only know how to use social media, they get story. Far from the apathetic creatures of caricature (elites would love us to believe that), many young people are seizing on "new" forms of communication to promote political change by any media necessary.[23]

Storytelling may be in vogue in campaigning circles, but as Sujatha Fernandes points out, we need to go beyond individualized accounts. Non-profits' use of personal stories in easily digestible soundbites mobilized toward narrow goals can disguise the real structural roots of inequality, defusing the confrontational politics of social movements.[24] As Sujatha argues, in an age in which the apparatus of narrative control has reached new levels of sophistication, through consumerism, corporate propaganda, political manipulation and full-scale information warfare:

We need stories that can win this battle. We need stories with whom people can identify – who invite our intended audiences to join them and enter the story as agents of change. We need stories with compelling villains who help us grasp the true nature of the dangers and threats we face. We need stories that foreshadow the world we know we can build together.[25]

As the stories told by elites crumble, these movements are contesting the old common sense and creating new ones. Telling a different story is vital to winning change and recruiting new rebels. The previous forms of solidarity on the left, most obviously trade unions, have been significantly eroded, deliberately so by the forces of the right. In the era of globalization, the absence of structures of solidarity leaves those left out susceptible to the exclusionary identities and false solidarity of right-wing populist appeals, or even worse. We need to build a better, more appealing common identity for change. We need a rebel alliance.

"How Do We Build the Rebellion from This?"

As Charles Derber suggests, we need to move beyond "silo activism" in order to build a universalizing resistance.[26] While issue-based activism plays an important role in identifying and fighting specific forms of injustice, it can sometimes fail to challenge the overall system that fuels almost all of the evils we're fighting.

Universalizing resistance is nonviolent and loving, but it refuses to let the system that threatens us continue as usual. It aims for a new society that moves beyond corporate oligarchy, authoritarianism, militarism, racism, sexism, homophobia and inequality in all its forms.

Similarly, veteran organizer George Lakey (*How We Win*) argues that protests and direct action need to develop into much larger campaigns – sustained and escalating sequences that grow connections for this new society and build a "movement of movements" with winnable demands to dislodge power.[27] This is the difference between mobilizing and organizing.

Paul Mason (*Why It's Kicking Off Everywhere*) notes the similarities between the current wave of resistance and the previous new left. Today's "spontaneous horizontalists" embrace a diversity of actors and fronts of struggle, a commitment to leaderless and prefigurative organizing (working in ways that reflect the society they want to build), grassroots democracy and consensus decision-making.[28] In a hierarchical world, they reflect Yoda's advice: "To answer power with power, the Jedi way this is not."

But Mason characterizes them as allergic to traditional politics. Jonathan Smucker (*Hegemony How-To: A Roadmap for Radicals*) agrees. Instead, progressives need to fight two battles simultaneously: for the ideas that drive political and media narratives (symbolic hegemony), and by building new organizations to support organizers, winning elected positions and contesting power in existing institutions (institutional hegemony).[29] The horizontal left might have won victories in symbolic hegemony, but isn't putting up enough of a fight for institutional hegemony, allowing corporations and the right free rein.

From a Marxist perspective, Nick Srnicek and Alex Williams (*Inventing the Future*) characterize much left-wing thinking in the West since the 1960s as "folk politics," aiming to bring politics down to the human scale via personal involvement in direct action, a focus on single issues and localism etc.[30] But these are insufficient to tackle global capitalism and neoliberalism. We have abandoned strategy, universalism, abstraction and the hard work of building workable global alternatives to capitalism. Instead, we need to learn from what neoliberals did over decades, building institutions and networks with the long-term aim of taking power.

The problem is, we haven't got this kind of time. Our crisis is here, now. Choices need to be made, but not false ones. In significant part thanks to Bernie Sanders' 2016 grassroots presidential campaign, the new new left is much more engaged in electoral and institutional politics. For the first time in a long time, we have hope. But far from being naive, the new new left's understandable distrust of existing institutions and recognition of the grip of elite financial power on politics means that pressure needs to be built and sustained externally as well.

As Micah White, co-creator of Occupy Wall Street, argues,

we are at the end of protest but the start of a new era of social change. Increasingly sophisticated movements will emerge in a bid to challenge elections, govern cities and change the way we live, while retaining a commitment to horizontalism, direct democracy and power sharing – perhaps even forming a global political party capable of winning elections worldwide.[31]

These movements, and so many others large and small, represent new ways of organizing and building communities for radical change. In *The Last Jedi*, Luke's most important lesson for Rey is that her relationship with the Force is more important than all of that Jedi lore. We can learn from the history of organizing and the left, but not become trapped by it. As Kate Aronoff puts it:

[T]oday's resistance needs fresh blood: new fighters and new strategies, but a new vision as well…If "The Last Jedi" has a political takeaway, it's for political revolution and a bottom-up transformation of not just who's in power, but who gets to decide how that revolution happens…Let your heroes and old dogmas die. Rebel scum have nothing to lose but their chains.[32]

"We Need a Statement, Not a Manifesto"

When we do engage in institutional politics, what do we propose? There's no point in not being bold, indeed if we're telling a story about the real challenges we face, timidity is not credible,

Healthcare for all. Free college. A massive jobs training program. A family wage. Affordable housing. Fundamental reform of policing, prisons and the criminal justice system. Reintroducing and expanding anti-monopoly laws. Dismantling the military-industrial complex. And critically, eradicating big money from politics. That's enough to be getting on with for the moment.

Long talked about in the left environmental movement,

the Green New Deal is now on the mainstream agenda. This incorporates growth in green tech, a jobs guarantee program, perhaps a universal basic income. The central significance of the Green New Deal is that it recognizes that confronting the environmental crises cannot be separated from social and economic fairness; its core linked principles are decarbonization, jobs and justice. It brings the sometimes abstract and technical "debate" over climate change down to what many people understand as immediate concerns and emphasizes the benefits of taking radical action. But it is also for the long-term; it sets out how we could achieve a just transition to a different kind of economy and society, and possibly avert some of the absolute worst of the climate disaster.

To the importance of the left reclaiming freedom, the Green New Deal would promote real liberties: freedom from fear (climate chaos and the social disasters a volatile planet could exacerbate); freedom from toil (less work, more fairly shared and less consumerism); freedom to move (genuinely sustainable transport, and to cope with inevitable climate displacement, solidarity without fences or walls); freedom from domination (from economic exploitation, racism, patriarchy and rampant resource extraction); and fundamentally, the freedom to live (to be able to meet our basic needs, but more than this, to live a good life).[33]

But on its own, the Green New Deal is not a story, none of these proposals are. Politics is first of all about engaging and motivating people to take their first steps into a larger world.

"I Need Someone to Show Me My Place in All This"
Some might still agree with DJ in *The Last Jedi* and his philosophy of not picking a side: "It's all a machine, partner. Live free, don't join." (Of course, he later betrays Finn and Rose to the First Order.) But we need to challenge such cynicism. As Wes Bishop states:

For all of its faults the...[the] Republic was not the Galactic Empire. Maddening bureaucracy, corruption, and endless argument and dispute was not the same as totalitarian rulers who destroyed entire planets...Merely saying the various political figures, political ideologies, and political parties are "all the same" because they are all produced by the same society is almost Sith like in its embrace of relativity."[34]

You might survive by taking DJ's stance, but being apolitical today has an even greater cost than when George Lucas was first developing his saga.[35] The walls of the trash compactor are closing in and we're all trapped inside. Yes, empire privileges some of us with comforts, but as Han said (though he meant it a different way), "What good's a reward if you ain't around to use it?"

What attracts us to fantasies such as *Star Wars* is that we'd like to believe that we too would join the Alliance and fight for freedom and justice, even if we come from a privileged background like Princess Leia. Perhaps we'd also like to think that we would have supported the civil rights movement, or the struggle against South Africa's apartheid regime, or any number of yesterday's causes. But would we? And what causes today might we look back on with shame that we didn't do more to support, because we didn't think they were our battles to fight? Perhaps we're more like Jyn Erso when she's challenged by rebel leader Saw Gerrera about whether she can stand to see the Imperial flag reign across the galaxy: "It's not a problem if you don't look up."

But confronting injustice demands first that we confront ourselves. As George Lucas once said:

The secret, ultimately, which is the bottom line in Star Wars and the other movies is there are two kinds of people in the world...Selfish people live on the dark side. The compassionate people live on the light side...Being selfish, following your pleasures...you're always going to be unhappy...You finally get everything you want and you're miserable because there's nothing at the end of that road, whereas if you are compassionate and you get to the end of the road, you've helped so many people.[36]

Far from glorifying individualism, *Star Wars* says that our individuality is an illusion. We are part of something bigger, we are all connected. The force is calling to us. We just need to let it in.

"You've Only Begun to Discover Your Power!"

Lucas also realized that audiences respond much more to optimism than bleak cynicism.[37] Hopelessness serves the ends of empire, but empire is losing. Writing before the sequel films, John Powers imagined how an *Episode VII* should provide hope, just as the OT did in its time:

It should offer young people a clear cut rebel victory; a much needed triumph for the real moral victories of the past thirty years. While the victories of the intervening years may seem modest compared to the great eras of reform; gay rights, environmentalism, and the on going gains of the women's movement are real victories that deserve a triumphal march. And while the US is still a bellicose power, more violent and war-like then any other industrialized nation, we are not as violent, or as racist, or as paranoid as we were thirty years ago. It isn't clear cut, but the rebels are winning.[38]

If at times we feel hopeless, it's because we forget that we are more powerful than we can possibly imagine. As Rebecca Solnit puts it in *Hope in the Dark*, we are a superpower whose nonviolent means are more powerful than violence, regimes and armies.[39] Empire knows this, just as in *The Empire Strikes Back* the Emperor warns Darth Vader that Luke "could destroy us." This is why mainstream media suggests that popular resistance is ridiculous, pointless or criminal (unless it's far far away, or a long time ago, or ideally both). This obscures the numerous nonviolent, direct action successes that are hidden in plain sight. We need to remind each other of the history of victories and transformations that give us the confidence that we can change the world, because we have many times before.

The collective story we call history is often written as if what happened was inevitable, but it wasn't. We don't know what is going to happen, or when. This uncertainty is the space of hope. And when it seems lacking, when the social depression that is capitalist realism seems all-pervasive, we still need to act.[40] Taking action often depends on faith in the absence of evidence that change is possible, since as Václav Havel wrote in *Disturbing the Peace*, "Hope is definitely not the same thing as optimism. It is not the conviction that something will turn out well, but the certainty that something makes sense, regardless of how it turns out."[41] Or as Vice Admiral Holdo says in *The Last Jedi*: "When I served under Leia, she always told me: 'Hope is like the sun. If you only believe in it when you can see it, you'll never make it through the night.'"

"In Every Corner of the Galaxy, the Downtrodden and Oppressed Know Our Symbol"

We noted in episode I that *Star Wars* is a story about stories, about the power of stories. The final illustration comes at the end of *The Last Jedi*.[42]

Luke gazes out at a double sunset on Ahch-To, echoing the first time we met him a long time ago on Tatooine, when he still dreamed of far-off adventures. Exhausted from projecting himself across the galaxy, Luke dies, giving himself to the Force. Cut to three slave children on the oligarch playground planet of

Canto Bight. One of them is telling the story of Luke's last stand and how he saved his comrades, acting it out with a homemade toy.

Suddenly the children are shooed away by their masters. The boy (his name is Temiri Blagg) goes outside. He grabs a broom and holds it like a lightsaber as it reflects the starlight. We see the ring given to him by Rose, as its Resistance symbol is revealed.[43]

One day the boy will be free, one day he will join the Rebellion and the fight for a better galaxy. High up in space a shooting star speeds across the sky, perhaps the spark that Poe Dameron predicts will light the fire that will burn the First Order down.

The Resistance is decimated, but there is still hope – in each other, and in a new generation who, inspired by stories of heroism, will find a way to join the rebellion and fight against oppression. Even the poorest stable boy is part of what happens next. What we do, and the stories we leave with others can, in ways we may never know, inspire them, and then others in turn...

Empires have been defeated before, and they always fall eventually. We can choose to remain subjects of an empire in crisis and collapse, or to live and act as citizens of a new republic, one we create through our actions big and small, starting here and now.

As the activist Chris Crass has said, we need to avoid being unconscious stormtroopers of death culture, helping imperial forces perpetuate systems of oppression. Instead, our calling is to see empire all around us, and to join a rebel alliance of others who are working to build a future of collective liberation and justice for all. As Luke says to Han: "Why don't you take a look around. You know what's about to happen, what they're up against. They could use a good pilot like you, you're turning your back on them."

The hero in us heeds the call to adventure. To live a life of fantasy today is not to escape into our favorite sci-fi films, so much as it is to believe that we can somehow escape from what empire is and what it is doing to our fellow human beings, to our planet and to ourselves. But there is still time, just about. Together, we can fulfill our destiny and become the guardians of peace and justice in our galaxy. Looking inside ourselves, we know we have already made our choice.

Welcome to the rebellion, _____ [write your name here]

"The Rebellion Is Reborn Today"

Like Luke at the beginning of *A New Hope*, we might think we're far from the action, toiling away in some backwater, and that the rebellion is far from here. Our daily responsibilities and chores take up all of our time and energy. It's not as if we like empire, but there's nothing we can do about it right now...

But maybe, like Luke and Biggs and many others, we also yearn for something more, a great adventure filled with purpose and meaning. Don't our hearts leap at the thought of rebelling and helping to build a new republic?

Our common morality tells us that empire – greed, domination, exploitation and rule by fear – is rotten. And such is its reach and ruthlessness, empire has now come for us. But whatever our position under its dominion, empire is not sustainable. It is more vulnerable than we often assume. The resistance is all around us, and it is spreading.

The *Star Wars* saga is about rebellion, but it's also about possibility in the face of enormous odds. It's this, not merchandizing or marketing or special effects, that really makes it so appealing. It's true that back in 1977 it provided audiences with a much-needed escape. But capitalism provides immeasurable means of escapism. What is it about *this* escape that has proved so popular and pervasive, passing down through generations and pulling in new audiences?

Star Wars was always political, and the saga will always be with us as long as there is oppression to be overturned and rebels who dream of doing it. As a fantasy, it connects with what is arguably the most real thing of all, even if we try to ignore it: the need to stand against domination and to fight for a better world. It's about how we find ourselves when we're confronted by what we must face down and defeat. That's the way we become the heroes of our lives, by being part of something much bigger, and sometimes much scarier. It's how we find camaraderie and fellowship and love as well. The force in ourselves, and the hope in each other.

Empire doesn't understand this. It fears that it will fall in the end, but it doesn't understand why. Because it doesn't understand hope, how hope sustains the rebellion that will eventually destroy it. How hope is not a choice, but an imperative.

As Denis Wood describes the scene at the end of *A New Hope*:

[I]t is a small crowd and a motley one and it is hidden in a cavern deep below the earth on a minor moon of a minor planet and the Starfleet is cruising in who knows what reaches of space and the Empire has not expired with the loss of a single battle station howsoever powerful…This is a small group of uncertain future of many kinds of peoples under the ground of a far-off foreign place. They are happy and proud for the moment, but Vader is alive, not only in a speeding fighter, but in all their hearts: tomorrow is another day, the future is uncertain, and the fight to stay truly alive in every sense of the word goes on.[1]

Endnotes

Prologue: "The Rebellion Is Spreading, And I Want to Be on the Side I Believe In"

1. Jamie Benning has produced an excellent "filmumentary," *Star Wars Begins*, that recuts *A New Hope* to include the deleted scenes, as well as voiceovers from cast and crew on the making of the film.

2. Moisture vaporators are a real thing. According to a paper published in *Science* in 2017, scientists from the University of California, Berkeley and the Massachusetts Institute of Technology have developed one which could work in the low humidity levels common in dry climates. In a climate changed world, this could be critical to ensuring that more people have access to clean water. See Hyunho Kim, Sungwoo Yang, Sameer R. Rao, Shankar Narayanan, Eugene A. Kapustin, Hiroyasu Furukawa, Ari S. Umans, Omar M. Yaghi, Evelyn N. Wang: "Water Harvesting from Air with Metal-organic Frameworks Powered by Natural Sunlight," *Science*, 28 April 2017, 356 (6336), pp 430-434.

3. The Empire runs academies across the galaxy to train recruits for the Imperial military. It's also often the only way for young people to escape desolate Outer Rim backwaters like Tatooine.

4. Luke and Biggs do meet again, at the Rebel base on Yavin just before the Rebels head off to attack the Death Star. The deleted scene better explains their joyful reunion and enhances the resonance of Biggs's later death in the battle.

5. George Lucas paid a fine and resigned from the Directors Guild rather than obey its demand that the film begin with normal opening credits. As we'll see, Lucas is a bit of a rebel.

6. A point made on the official *Star Wars* website by Eric Gellner: "Corruption, Exploitation, and Decay: The Politics of Star Wars," *Star Wars*, November 6, 2012.

7. This might seem like a clear indication that the Empire is totalitarian-socialist, indeed some conservative commentators have picked up

on this scene to suggest this. However, as we'll see, George Lucas was far more concerned with the threat of authoritarian capitalism.

8. Whereas the original film trilogy emphasizes the machinations of the evil Emperor, the novelization takes a more institutional approach, in which the Galactic Republic was corrupted from within by greedy corporate interests and power-hungry bureaucrats. These themes re-emerge in the prequel trilogy.

Episode I: "Many of the Truths We Cling to Depend Greatly on Our Own Point of View"

1. For an excellent account of how fake stories are designed to unmoor people from reality and lead them to authoritarianism, see Timothy Snyder: *The Road to Unfreedom: Russia, Europe, America* (New York: Tim Duggan Books, 2018). As Adam Curtis notes in his documentary *HyperNormalisation*, science fiction fan and would-be theater director Vladislav Surkov has helped Vladimir Putin use the media to generate a climate of confusion and contradiction, manipulating the Russian people to turn to the Kremlin for reassurance and "stability" (as we'll see, somewhat like Senator Palpatine's tactics in *Star Wars*). It turns out that postmodern storytelling, in which no truth is certain, can induce defeatism and serve despotism; see also Peter Pomerantsev: *Nothing Is True and Everything Is Possible: The Surreal Heart of the New Russia* (New York: PublicAffairs, 2015).

2. Yuval Noah Harari suggests that public faith in the "liberal story" collapsed because of the global financial crisis, exacerbated by the accelerating pace of technological disruption, hence the disorientation among liberal elites, Yuval Noah Harari: *21 Lessons for the 21st Century* (London: Jonathan Cape, 2018), particularly "Part 1: The Technological Challenge, 1 Disillusionment. The End of History Has Been Postponed." But as Adam Curtis points out in *HyperNormalisation*, at least for a time in the 1990s, as conservative thinkers proclaimed the "end of history" and center-left parties adopted the neoliberal consensus, mainstream politicians stopped

telling any stories at all. This opened the way for Trump et al to create their new fictions.

3. Arlie Russell Hochschild: *Strangers in Their Own Land: Anger and Mourning on the American Right* (New York and London: The New Press, 2018). As pointed out by Francesca Polletta, author of *It Was Like a Fever: Storytelling in Protest and Politics*, and Jessica Callahan, many elements of the deep story should not have made sense. Many of Hoschild's respondents have been the beneficiaries of federal programs. Few had lost out on jobs and opportunities to immigrants or people of color. They also seemed to know very few liberals. To Polletta and Callahan, such is the power of storytelling to shape reality; Francesca Polletta and Jessica Callahan: "Deep Stories, Nostalgia Narratives, and Fake News: Storytelling in the Trump Era," in: *American Journal of Cultural Sociology*, 2017, pp 2049-7113.

4. As Steve Almond suggests, Trump's bad story built on many previous bad stories, including enduring pathologies of race, class, immigration and tribalism. Steve Almond: *Bad Stories: What the Hell Just Happened to Our Country* (Pasadena: Red Hen Press, 2018).

5. Arlie Russell Hochschild: *Strangers in Their Own Land: Anger and Mourning on the American Right* (New York: The New Press, 2018), p 14.

6. This said, the evidence suggests that Trump's victory was much more about race and identity, which is to say culture and stories, specifically white supremacy, than it was primarily about economic issues; see Ta-Nehisi Coates: "The First White President," *The Atlantic*, October 2017.

7. Echoing the points made about the hard-right's stories, the stories the Sith tell in *Star Wars* may be manipulations but they contain some truths: Darth Vader's revelation about who his son is, Darth Sideous' tale about Darth Plagueis, Count Dooku's criticisms of the Republic's corruption, and so on.

8. In dramatic terms, these conflicting stories also set up the confrontation between Luke and Vader at the climax of *Return of*

the Jedi. Does Darth Vader still contain some remnant of Anakin Skywalker, as Luke hopes, or has he been wholly consumed by the dark side, as Kenobi, Vader and the Emperor maintain? As we'll see in episode II, this conflict also serves a political purpose in the story.

9. Jonathan Gottschall: *The Storytelling Animal, How Stories Make Us Human* (Boston and New York: Mariner Books, 2013).

10. Yuval Noah Harari: *Sapiens: A Brief History of Humankind* (New York: HarperCollins, 2015).

11. David Brin and Matthew Woodring Stover: *Star Wars on Trial: Science Fiction and Fantasy Writers Debate the Most Popular Science Fiction Films of All Time* (Dallas: BenBella Books, 2006), p 2-3, 4.

12. A nice simple definition offered by Lisa Cron: *Wired for Story, The Writer's Guide to Using Brain Science to Hook Readers from the Very First Sentence* (New York: Ten Speed Press, 2012).

13. As described by perhaps the most famous modern story guru Robert McKee: *Story: Style, Structure, Substance, and the Principles of Screenwriting* (New York: HarperCollins, 1997). Stanley Kubrick made a similar point about what was most important in film storytelling: emotional logic, flow, not rational logic.

14. Orlando D'Adamo: "How Storytelling Explains World Politics, from Spain to the US," *The Conversation*, February 6, 2017.

15. David Ricci puts this down to liberals' "post-Enlightenment disenchantment," David Ricci: *Politics without Stories: The Liberal Predicament* (New York: Cambridge University Press, 2016).

16. See Robert Reich: "Donald Trump Tells A Fake American Story. We Must Tell the Real One," *The Guardian*, March 4, 2019.

17. However, George Monbiot argues that left and right have both been using a restoration story to diminishing and dangerous returns. For the center-left, this has been "a microwaved version of the remnants of Keynesian social democracy." But this old story has lost most of its content and narrative force because the program buckled in response to the political demands of capital and now because it collides with environmental crisis. We return

to this point in episode IV. George Monbiot: "How Do We Get Out of this Mess?," *The Guardian*, September 9, 2017.

18. A significant body of research on political communication demonstrates that this isn't just about evidence, more often it's about values and emotions. We think using "frames," mental structures that allow us to understand reality and sometimes to create what we take to be reality. Perhaps the best-known proponent of this view is George Lakoff, who has been called the "father of framing"; see George Lakoff: *Don't Think of an Elephant! Know Your Values and Frame the Debate* (Hartford: Chelsea Green Publishing, 2004); also Drew Westen: *The Political Brain, The Role of Emotion in Deciding the Fate of the Nation* (New York: Public Affairs, 2007).

19. As we'll see in episode III, this does not mean that the left can't tell a story about how aspects of the past were better. There was more security for ordinary people before the new right further entrenched wealth and power in elites. But we can also tell a bigger story about restoring a more fundamental balance, as discussed in episode V.

20. Yves Citton: *Mythocratie, Storytelling et Imaginaire de Gauche* (Paris: Editions Amsterdam, 2010).

21. George Monbiot: *Out of the Wreckage: A New Politics for an Age of Crisis* (London: Verso, 2017).

22. Yves Citton: "Populism and the Empowering Circulation of Myths," *The Populist Imagination*, Open 2010, 20.

23. Stephen Duncombe: *Dream: Re-imagining Progressive Politics in an Age of Fantasy* (New York and London: The New Press, 2007).

24. Another irony: the resulting cultural studies in the US and UK further developed under the influence of the new left in the 1960s, but as we'll see in the next episode, *Star Wars* was fundamentally a new left story about anti-authoritarianism and liberation.

25. Theodor Adorno and Max Horkheimer: *Dialectic of Enlightenment* (New York: Continuum, 1947).

26. Theodor Adorno and Max Horkheimer: *Dialectic of Enlightenment*

(New York: Continuum, 1947), p 100.

27. Theodor Adorno: *Minima Moralia: Reflections from Damaged Life* (London and New York: Verso, 1951/2005), p 206.

28. Jean-François Lyotard: *The Postmodern Condition: A Report on Knowledge* (Manchester: Manchester University Press, 1979/1984).

29. Ellen Meiksins Wood: "Modernity, Postmodernity or Capitalism?," *Review of International Political Economy*, 4: 3, 1997, pp 539-560.

30. Andreas Malm: *The Progress of This Storm: Nature and Society in a Warming World* (London: Verso Futures, 2018).

31. Most prominently in Hannah Arendt: *The Human Condition* (Chicago: University of Chicago Press, 1958, 2nd edn.).

32. Stephen Duncombe: *Dream: Re-imagining Progressive Politics in an Age of Fantasy* (New York and London: The New Press, 2007), p 174.

33. Walidah Imarisha and adrienne maree brown (eds): *Octavia's Brood: Science Fiction Stories from Social Justice Movements* (Oakland and Edinburgh: AK Press, 2015), p 3.

34. Or as Kevin Smith calls Episodes IV-VI, The Holy Trinity.

35. Mark Fisher: *Capitalist Realism: Is There No Alternative?* (London: Zero Books, 2009).

36. As defined by Wolfgang Streeck: *How Will Capitalism End? Essays on a Failing System* (London: Verso, 2016).

37. Mark Fisher: *Ghosts of My Life: Writings on Depression, Hauntology and Lost Futures* (London: Zero Books, 2014). This echoes Fredric Jameson's critique of *Star Wars* as a nostalgia film. It satisfies a longing to re-experience not the past as such (since the events of the saga are not actual intergalactic history), but our own past through forms such as Buck Rogers serials; see Fredric Jameson: "Postmodernism and Consumer Society," pp 1-20, *The Cultural Turn, Selected Writings on the Postmodern 1983-1998* (London: Verso, 1998).

38. Chris Crass: "Jedis for Collective Liberation: Why a Multiracial Star Wars Matters," The Anarres Project for Alternative Futures, October 20, 2015.

39. Ajmal Khattak: "A Rebel History of Star Wars," *Spectre*, May 25,

2016.

40. Bloch's book on the rise of fascism in the 1930s, *Heritage of Our Times*, attacked both the orthodox Marxist left and his friends in the Frankfurt school for not realizing that fascism was a perverted religious movement which won people over with quasi-utopian ideas about the wonders of a future Reich. In other words, perversely, even fascism is a form of hope. Ernst Bloch: *Heritage of Our Times* (Polity Press: Cambridge, 1962/1991).

41. A point made by Francesca Polletta: "Storytelling in Politics," *Contexts*, 7: 4, 2008, pp 26-31.

42. Kate Aronoff: "Star Wars Goes to the Countryside," *Jacobin*, December 17, 2016.

43. David Mark: "For Some US Adults, Star Wars and Politics Just Don't Mix," *Morning Consult*, December 6, 2017.

44. Ajmal Khattak: "A Rebel History of Star Wars," *Spectre*, May 25, 2016.

45. Denis Wood: "The Stars in Our Hearts – A Critical Commentary on George Lucas' Star Wars," *Journal of Popular Film*, 6 (3), pp 262-279.

46. A point made by Ronald Aronson: *We: Reviving Social Hope* (Chicago: University of Chicago Press, 2017).

Episode II: "Rebellions Are Built on Hope"

1. J. W. Rinzler: *The Making of Star Wars (Enhanced Edition)* (New York: Ballantine Books), p 16.

2. Will Brooker: *Star Wars BFI Film Classics* (London: Palgrave Macmillan, 2009), p 8.

3. Pauline Kael: "Contrasts," The Current Cinema, *The New Yorker*, September 26, 1977. In lamenting the film's energy, Kael echoes Adorno and Horkheimer's miserablism: "[Films] are so designed that quickness, powers of observation, and experience are undeniably needed to apprehend them at all; yet sustained thought is out of the question if the spectator is not to miss the relentless rush of facts." Theodor Adorno and Max Horkheimer: *Dialectic of Enlightenment* (New York: Continuum, 1947), pp 126-127.

4.   As described by writer/filmmaker Phil Cousineau, who has helped to promote Joseph Campbell's work on the journey of the archetypal hero shared by world mythologies (the monomyth); Joseph Campbell, Phil Cousineau (ed): *The Hero's Journey, Joseph Campbell on His Life and Work* (Novato: New World Library, 2003). Campbell's influence on *Star Wars* was first promoted by Andrew Gordon: "Star Wars: A Myth for Our Time," *Literature/ Film Quarterly*, 6: 4, Fall 1978, pp 314-326, although the film critic Roger Ebert also referred to the hero's journey in his 1977 review of *A New Hope*, see Roger Ebert: *Star Wars*. However, this influence has probably been overstated, perhaps adding to the neglect of *Star Wars'* political motivations.

5.   Denis Wood: *The Time of the Stars* (unpublished, 1978).

6.   Garry Jenkins: *Empire Building: The Remarkable Real Life Story of Star Wars* (New York: Citadel Press, 1999), p 167.

7.   As quoted by Will Brooker: *Star Wars BFI Film Classics* (London: Palgrave Macmillan, 2009), p 13.

8.   See the documentary *The People vs. George Lucas* (2010), in which fans bemoan many of Lucas's decisions while paying homage to the power and impact of the original films.

9.   Jase Short: "The Substance of Geek Culture," *Jacobin*, September 24, 2013.

10. Indeed, as Jason Rothery suggests, "This process of consumption, appropriation, and cross-pollination – of *play* – is how *Star Wars* became "myth" in the truest sense of the word – an ahistorical, multi-authored "open access" text perpetually (re-)appropriated for (re-)interpretation and transfiguration." Jason Rothery: *A Tale of Two Trilogies: Severing the Star Wars Saga*, 2012, p 139.

11. Andrey Summers: "The Complex and Terrifying Reality of Star Wars Fandom," *Jive*, May 31, 2005.

12. As quoted in Ajmal Khattak: "A Rebel History of Star Wars," *Spectre*, May 25, 2016.

13. As quoted in Benjamin Hufbauer: "The Politics Behind the Original 'Star Wars,'" *Los Angeles Review of Books*, December 21, 2015.

14. As quoted in Benjamin Hufbauer: "The Politics Behind the Original 'Star Wars,'" *Los Angeles Review of Books*, December 21, 2015.

15. George Lucas, "Foreword," in Jonathan Bresman: *MAD About Star Wars* (New York: Del Ray, 2007).

16. Camille Paglia: "George Lucas's Force," *The Chronicle of Higher Education*, October 15, 2015.

17. Richard Grenier: "Celebrating Defeat," *Commentary*, August 1980.

18. Mark Fisher: *Capitalist Realism: Is There No Alternative?* (London: Zero Books, 2009), p 14.

19. Michael Ryan and Douglas Kellner: *Camera Politica: Politics and Ideology in Contemporary Hollywood Film* (Bloomington and Indianapolis: Indiana University Press, 1988).

20. Perhaps the first time this type of analysis was put forward was by Karen Winter, "The Politics of STAR WARS," *Organia*, 1981, albeit that Winter interprets the saga as an appeal for a return to the libertarian political philosophy of an earlier America.

21. To the Marxist philosopher Slavoj Žižek it is precisely because you can interpret the saga in different ways that makes it an effective political myth. Slavoj Žižek: "Revenge of Global Finance," *In These Times*, May 21, 2005.

22. Tom Engelhardt: *The End of Victory Culture: Cold War America and the Disillusioning of a Generation* (Amherst: University of Massachusetts Press, 2007, revised edition). A similar point is made by former Marine Roy Scranton: "'Star Wars' and the Fantasy of American Violence," *The New York Times*, July 2, 2016.

23. Mumia Abu-Jamal: "Star Wars and the American Imagination," in Walidah Imarisha and adrienne maree brown (eds): *Octavia's Brood: Science Fiction Stories from Social Justice Movements* (Oakland and Edinburgh: AK Press, 2015), p 255-258.

24. Ty Burr: "George Lucas Interview," *Boston Globe*, undated.

25. Lucas also used bits of old black and white Second World War films to give skeptical studio bosses a sense of how the space battles would feel, and the Death Star trench run was inspired by the likes of *The Dam Busters* and *633 Squadron*.

26. Lucas cast the horror icon Peter Cushing in the role of Grand Moff Tarkin, helping to emphasize the inherent evilness of the Empire, and repeated this with Christopher (Dracula) Lee's role as Count Dooku/Darth Tyranus in *Attack of the Clones* and *Revenge of the Sith*.

27. A medical exam later revealed that Lucas had diabetes, which meant that he would have avoided the draft anyway.

28. J. W. Rinzler: *The Making of Star Wars (Enhanced Edition)* (New York: Ballantine Books), p 8.

29. Arthur Chrenkoff: "Star Wars Has Always Been a Leftie Fantasy," *The Spectator Australia*, December 20, 2017.

30. John Powers: "Star Wars and Postmodernism," *Star Wars Modern*, March 7, 2011.

31. Salar Mohandesi, Bjarke Skaerlund Risager, and Laurence Cox (eds): *Voices of 1968: Documents from the Global North* (London: Pluto Press, 2018).

32. Richard Vinen: *The Long '68: Radical Protest and Its Enemies* (London: Allen Lane, 2018).

33. As described by Salar Mohandesi, Bjarke Skaerlund Risager and Laurence Cox (eds): *Voices of 1968: Documents from the Global North* (London: Pluto Press, 2018).

34. Richard Vinen: *The Long '68: Radical Protest and Its Enemies* (London: Allen Lane, 2018).

35. As quoted in Clara Bingham: *Witness to the Revolution: Radicals, Resisters, Vets, Hippies, and the Year America Lost Its Mind and Found Its Soul* (New York: Random House, 2016), p xxxiv.

36. As Laurence Cox has noted, "These struggles remade the landscape of social movements and popular resistance for decades to come: Autonomia and Situationism, a rainbow of feminisms, anarchism and Trotskyism, black and indigenous activism, counter-cultural and lesbian/gay movements offered new ways of thinking grounded in radical struggle. The moment in which social relationships were laid bare and it was possible to imagine a world beyond capitalism, patriarchy and the racial global order still resonates today as an experience of revolutionary possibility." Laurence Cox: "How

Events in 1968 Reshaped the World," *New Frame*, January 21, 2019. We consider the new new left in episode V.

37. Douglas Murphy: *Last Futures: Nature, Technology and the End of Architecture* (London: Verso, 2016).

38. As quoted in Benjamin Hufbauer: "The Politics Behind the Original 'Star Wars,'" *Los Angeles Review of Books*, December 21, 2015.

39. Dave Schilling: "Star Wars: The Last Jedi Review: The Star Wars Film That Finally Lives Up To Empire Strikes Back," *Birth.Movies. Death*, December 12, 2017.

40. John Powers: "Thoughts on Episode VII: 'Something something something DARKSIDE something something something COMPLETE,'" Star Wars Modern, November 19, 2012.

41. As Amedeo D'Adamo puts it: "...when we step back to view Deathstarchitecture's marriage of sterile institution, opaque rational instrumental purpose, corporate maze and pure work space, a larger and more powerful emotional logic to the Death Star becomes obvious. We long to destroy such places." Amedeo D'Adamo: "Deathstarchitecture: The Space of Evil," *Kinephanos*, 8: 1, June 2018.

42. Audio commentary to *Star Wars Episode III: Revenge of the Sith* (DVD, Lucasfilm, 2005). Similarly, Lucas said that "It isn't that the Empire conquered the Republic. It's that the Empire *is* the Republic." As quoted in Richard Corliss and Jess Cagle: "Dark Victory," *Time*, April 29, 2002.

43. As nicely summarized by Nader Elhefnawy: "In Defense of the Star Wars Prequels, Part II," *Raritania*, August 27, 2013

44. As quoted in Today: "Cannes Embraces Political Message in 'Star Wars,'" *Today*, May 16, 2005. But as you might expect of the prosecutor of *Star Wars on Trial*, David Brin is a skeptic, see David Brin and Matthew Woodring Stover: *Star Wars on Trial: Science Fiction and Fantasy Writers Debate the Most Popular Science Fiction Films of All Time* (Dallas: BenBella Books, 2006). Brin actually loves the first two (OT) films: he thinks that *A New Hope* "expressed unadulterated joy" and *The Empire Strikes Back* is "inarguably one

of the most beautiful and inspiring science fiction films ever made." But particularly with regards to the prequel trilogy, he complains that Lucas never shows the Republic functioning. Yet that's surely the point: how flawed republics become dysfunctional and prey to authoritarianism.

45. Anne Lancashire: "*Attack of the Clones* and the Politics of *Star Wars*," *The Dalhousie Review*, 82: 2, 2002, pp 235-253. Militarism infects everyone. During the Clone Wars, the Jedi are appointed as military generals, becoming complicit in the war against the Separatists. Further, as a result of the Clone Wars (as depicted in the animated TV series), many of the Republic's social services, including education, infrastructure, healthcare and basic amenities, suffered from budget cuts. The Republic was dragged to the verge of bankruptcy.

46. Maureen Dowd: "The Aura of Arugulance," *The New York Times*, April 18, 2009.

47. As Jase Short notes, tie-ins such as the novels and comics paint a backdrop to *The Force Awakens* that expands on the thin politics of the film: the Rebellion transforms into the New Republic, a peace treaty is signed with Imperial remnants, but Princess Leia forms a Resistance (publicly disavowed by the New Republic but secretly supported by several Senators) due to her fear that the Empire will re-emerge. See Jase Short: "The Cultural Economy of Star Wars," *Red Wedge*, April 14, 2016.

48. Then again, you can regard the First Order as a kind of Empire redux, a hyper-ideological movement but without a clear sense of purpose, rather like today's harder right that has taken over the Republican Party and conservatism more broadly.

49. One respect in which the *Star Wars* universe remains unrepresentative is in its paucity of LGBTQ characters. As Alex Acks suggests, queer people have been exiled to the margins, which is ironic given that the Empire takes worlds and destroys their diversity; Alex Acks: "Star Wars: Still Disappointingly Heterosexual," *Book Riot*, June 12, 2017. Chuck Wendig, author of the *Star Wars: Aftermath* trilogy

which included a gay leading character, was fired from (Disney-owned) Marvel projects for his tweets criticizing the Republican Party. Wendig responded to review-bombers of *Aftermath* thus: "You're not the Rebel Alliance. You're not the good guys. You're the fucking Empire, man. You're the shitty, oppressive, totalitarian Empire...Stop being the Empire. Join the Rebel Alliance. We have love and inclusion and great music and cute droids." Chuck Wendig: "Star Wars: Aftermath – Reviews, News, and Such!" *Chuck Wendig: TerribleMinds*, September 7, 2015.

50. Brin argues that from *The Return of the Jedi* and especially the prequels, *Star Wars* reflects the great man theory of history, especially in the notion that (Jedi) elites have an inherent right to arbitrary rule; see David Brin and Matthew Woodring Stover: *Star Wars on Trial: Science Fiction and Fantasy Writers Debate the Most Popular Science Fiction Films of All Time* (Dallas: BenBella Books, 2006).

51. Toby Moses: "Anti-Empire, Pro-activist...The Last Jedi is as Left Wing as Jeremy Corbyn," *The Guardian*, December 19, 2017.

52. The male-dominated Empire is also quite happy to torture women who dare to resist, starting with Leia in *A New Hope* and echoed with Rey in *The Last Jedi*. No doubt under considerable corporate pressure, Weitz later apologized and deleted the tweet, while Disney denied that a film about a galactic rebellion is in any way political.

53. Pauline Kael: "Blade Runner: Baby, The Rain Must Fall," The New Yorker, July 12, 1982, p 82.

54. Jill Lepore: "A Golden Age for Dystopian Fiction," *The New Yorker*, June 5 and 12, 2017.

55. Cass R. Sunstein: *The World According to Star Wars* (New York: HarperCollins, 2016), p 6. As Sunstein notes, in *The Empire Strikes Back*, faced with the temptation to join the dark side and gain unlimited power, Luke leaps into the abyss. To Sunstein, this is perhaps the greatest example of free will.

56. Denis Wood: *The Time of the Stars* (unpublished, 1978).

57. More accurately, *Star Wars* has reflected the gender politics of the time. *A New Hope* carried science fiction into the second wave feminist era, albeit inconsistently, but then came the backlash into post-feminism, the prequels' somewhat superficial girl power and now the sequels (and spin-offs) with more female leads as respected fighters and equal partners with male characters; see Valerie Estelle Frankel: *Star Wars Meets the Eras of Feminism: Weighing All the Galaxy's Women Great and Small* (London: Lexington Books, 2018).

58. As noted by Sarah E. Parkinson, Aronson assistant professor of political science and international studies at Johns Hopkins University; Sarah E. Parkinson: "How to Watch Star Wars Like an Insurgent," *The Washington Post*, December 15, 2017. In *A New Hope*, Leia is the first of the main characters to have joined the Rebellion; she's also the only one mentioned in the opening text crawl. It was appropriate then that Leia memes were prominent in the #Resist demonstrations following Donald Trump's election and in the Women's March in January 2017, the largest protest in US history.

59. As quoted by Chris Taylor: "Star Wars is Political, and It Always Has Been," *Mashable*, November 23, 2016.

60. Howard Zinn: *A Power Governments Cannot Suppress* (San Francisco: City Lights Books, 2007), p 270.

Episode III: "Nothing Will Stand in Our Way"

1. Becky Sharp provides a good summary of this conservative *Star Wars*. Becky Sharp: "Star Wars Politics Part Two: The Right Side Strikes Back," *Retrozap*. November 7, 2016.

2. In 1983, the year of *Return of the Jedi*, the administration's space-bound anti-missile Strategic Defense Initiative was also quickly nicknamed "Star Wars" by critics. Lucasfilm sued lobbyists for using his film's title (Reagan also disliked his program being belittled), but Lucasfilm lost the case. Due to its ubiquity, "Star Wars" had become a common term for political commentary.

3. Jonathan V. Last: "The Case for the Empire," *The Weekly Standard*, May 15, 2002.

4. As quoted in Asawin Suebsaeng: "Why Conservatives Love the Galactic Empire," *Daily Beast*, October 20, 2015.

5. Sonny Bunch: "The Destruction of Alderaan was Completely Justified," *The Washington Post*, October 29, 2015. For a much, much better level of analysis, see Max Brooks, John Amble, ML Cavanaugh and Jaym Gates (eds), *Strategy Strikes Back: How Star Wars Explains Modern Military Conflict* (Lincoln: Potomac Books, 2018).

6. David French: "In the Battle of Jedi Versus Sith, I'll Take the Sith Every Time," *National Review*, October 21, 2015.

7. Ron Suskind: "Without a Doubt," *The New York Times Magazine*, October 17, 2004, p 51.

8. As quoted by Michael Wolff: "Ringside with Steve Bannon at Trump Tower as the President-Elect's Strategist Plots 'An Entirely New Political Movement' (Exclusive)," *The Hollywood Reporter*, November 18, 2016.

9. Kate Aronoff: "Star Wars Goes to the Countryside," *Jacobin*, December 17, 2016.

10. As Lucas said, politics was always intrinsic to *Star Wars*, "…it's just that most people never noticed it until [Sith] was put into the puzzle. Sometimes the politics are kind of confused and muddled in terms of the way people see [them], which is the way most people see politics." (Audio commentary, *Revenge of the Sith*, DVD, Lucasfilm, 2005).

11. Lucas was topical in talking about trade. The year 1999, when *The Phantom Menace* was released, was also the year of the anti-globalization protests at the World Trade Organization meeting in Seattle and the publication of Naomi Klein's *No Logo*. Writing in the *Los Angeles Times*, Andrei Cherny, a former speechwriter for Vice President Al Gore, thought that Lucas was expressing similar concerns about international trade and the declining autonomy of national governments (for which read the planet Naboo), and warned against what he saw as rising calls for "protectionism"; Andrei Cherny: "The Scary Politics of 'The Phantom Menace,'" *Los*

Angeles Times, May 30, 1999.

12. Nancy MacLean: *Democracy in Chains: The Deep History of the Radical Right's Stealth Plan for America* (New York: Penguin Books, 2017).

13. Robert Kuttner: *Can Democracy Survive Global Capitalism?* (New York: W. W. Norton & Company, 2018).

14. Indeed, George Lucas began the second draft of the script of *A New Hope* from January 1975 (retained in the third draft) with the following opening crawl: "The REPUBLIC GALACTICA is dead. Ruthless trader barons, driven by greed and the lust for power, have replaced enlightenment with oppression, and 'rule by the people' with the FIRST GALACTIC EMPIRE."

15. Nader Elhefnawy: "In Defense of the Star Wars Prequels, Part II," *Raritania*, August 27, 2013.

16. As even *The New York Times* has noted, the defining political fact of our time is not polarization but how majority views are ignored, for example support for higher taxes on the rich, paid maternity leave, net neutrality and stronger privacy laws. Entire categories of public policy options are off-limits because of the combined influence of industry and donors on Congress. Tim Wu: "The Oppression of the Supermajority," *The New York Times*, March 5, 2019.

17. Michael O'Connor: "Sounding Like a Separatist: Star Wars Politics," *Retrozap*, November 7, 2016. Reviewing *Attack of the Clones*, David Begor also notices that: "[T]he Dark Side is always mired in the language of commerce, an association strengthened through its reliance on bounty hunters and smugglers, and reinforced more subtly through the use of casual references to "deals" and "bargains" that backfire continually on those who make them." David Begor: "Defense of the Clones: Lucas's Latest: Cheap Thrills or Sophisticated Filmmaking?," *Bright Lights*, November 1, 2002

18. Jason Ward: "Star Wars & Neoliberalism: Lucasfilm's Critique of Free Market Capitalism," *Making Star Wars*, August 6, 2013.

19. As Jason notes, Lucas had more to say about the effects of unbridled capitalism on democracy in his TV spin-off *The Clone*

Wars. Echoing David Harvey in *A Brief History of Neoliberalism*, the series repeatedly depicts neoliberalism's "accumulation through dispossession" – the privatization of things that once belonged to the people – as central to Imperial domination, of public immiseration and private power.

20. Wookieepedia: "Dissolution of the Imperial Senate," undated.

21. The rich *have* bought government. Professors Martin Gilens and Ben Page studied 1779 instances of proposed policy changes between 1981 and 2002. They found that economic elites and organized groups representing business interests have substantial independent impacts on US government policy, while average citizens and mass-based interest groups have little or no independent influence. Martin Gilens and Ben Page: "Testing Theories of American Politics: Elites, Interest Groups, and Average Citizens," *Perspectives on Politics*, September 2014. Gilens has also found that the policy preferences of the rich are 15 times more likely to become public policy as those of non-elites; Martin Gilens: *Affluence and Influence: Economic Inequality and Political Power in America* (Princeton: Princeton University Press, 2012).

22. Bauman, Zygmunt: *In Search of Politics* (Cambridge: Polity, 1999), Introduction.

23. Boldly, Lucas once said in an interview that with *Star Wars* he was "telling an old myth in a new way. Each society takes that myth and retells it...which relates to the particular environment they live in. The motif is the same. It's just that it gets localized. As it turns out, I'm localizing it for the planet." Bill Moyers and George Lucas: "Of Myth and Men," *Time*, April 18, 1999.

24. Kevin J. Wetmore Jr. explores the first argument in *The Empire Triumphant*, a postcolonial critique of the saga; Kevin J. Wetmore, Jr.: *The Empire Triumphant: Race, Religion and Rebellion in the Star Wars Films* (Jefferson and London: McFarland & Company, 2005). The Rebellion is predominantly white, in contrast to real-world rebellions led by people of color against colonial powers such as the British Empire. Relatedly, albeit humorously, in Kevin Smith's

Chasing Amy the black gay comic book writer Hooper LaMante, a.k.a Hooper X, suggests that the Rebellion represents the violent white gentrification of the galaxy. *Star Wars* is also accused of appropriating Asian culture (for example, Japanese folktales and cinema) but offering it up as alien, as well as non-Westerners literally being depicted as aliens.

25. As suggested by Mark Thornton regarding *The Phantom Menace* on the libertarian Mises Institute blog, Mark Thornton: "Star Wars Revisited," Mises Institute, August 7, 1990.

26. Kevin J. Wetmore, Jr.: *The Empire Triumphant: Race, Religion and Rebellion in the Star Wars Films* (Jefferson and London: McFarland & Company, 2005). In fact, the Sith's imperialism goes back way further than depicted in the films. Shortly after being banished from the newly formed Republic with the help of the Jedi Knights, the Sith Lords built a massive Old Sith Empire. In response, the Republic and the Jedi militarized. A succession of conflicts between the two led eventually to the Sith's defeat. The Jedi wiped out the rest of the Sith except for Darth Bane, who established the Rule of Two, leading to the ascension of Darth Sidious.

27. M. Keith Booker: *Alternate Americas: Science Fiction Film and American Culture* (Westport and London: Praeger, 2006), pp 116, 118. Further to this view, Michael O'Connor ties together the generational and anti-imperialist interpretations of *Star Wars*: "[T]he Empire was the older generation, the fathers who supposedly knew best. Britain had been America's father before the Revolutionary War; now Lucas was encouraging a second rebellion. This time it was directed against the previous generation who had exploited America's post-war power and prosperity by forcing its will on the rest of the world." Michael O'Connor: "Sounding Like A Separatist: Star Wars Politics," *Retrozap*, November 7, 2016.

28. Niall Ferguson: *Empire: How Britain Made the Modern World* (London: Allen Lane, 2003), p xix.

29. This was a long-standing fear in American politics which significantly pre-dates the new left. For example, in 1902 Brooks

148

Adams, the American historian, political scientist and critic of capitalism, prophesied in *The New Empire* that Europe and Great Britain would soon become dependencies of an American empire of commerce.

30. Haseeb Ahmed with Chris Cutrone: "Interview with Slavoj Žižek: The Occupy Movement, a Renascent Left, and Marxism Today," *Platypus Review*, 42, December 2011 – January 2012.

31. Michael Hardt and Antonio Negri: *Empire* (Cambridge: Harvard University Press, 2001), p 324.

32. Michael Hardt and Antonio Negri: *Empire* (Cambridge: Harvard University Press, 2001), p xv.

33. Michael O'Connor: "Sounding Like A Separatist: Star Wars Politics," *Retrozap*, November 7, 2016.

34. As quoted in Tyler Cowen: "Cass Sunstein on Judicial Minimalism, the Supreme Court, and Star Wars (Ep. 10-Live)," *Conversations With Tyler/Medium*, June 22, 2016.

35. Like the transition from Republic to Empire in *Star Wars*, to Steven Levitsky and Daniel Ziblatt democracy no longer ends with a bang, in revolutions or military coups, but with a whimper, the slow, steady weakening of institutions such as the judiciary and the press, and the erosion of long-standing political norms. According to Levitsky and Ziblatt, Donald Trump meets all four criteria for an authoritarian-style leader; Steven Levitsky and Daniel Ziblatt: *How Democracies Die* (New York: Broadway Books, 2018).

36. David Neiwert: *Alt-America: The Rise of the Radical Right in the Age of Trump* (London: Verso, 2019).

37. Naomi Klein: *No Is Not Enough: Resisting Trump's Shock Politics and Winning the World We Need* (London: Penguin, 2017).

38. As quoted in Richard Corliss and Jess Cagle: "Dark Victory," *Time*, April 29, 2002

39. There were those who strived to restore the democratic ideals and institutions of the Republic, in recognition that a government dominated by monied interests and unreceptive to the needs of the people would be at risk of the lure of autocracy. They included

Padmé Amidala, Bail Organa (Leia's adopted father) and future Rebel Alliance leader Mon Mothma. As seen in *The Clone Wars* TV series, during what would be the last years of the Republic this group fought for measures such as regulation of the Banking Clan, while demanding that the voice of ordinary citizens be heard. Of course, they would fail.

40. As quoted in Ishaan Tharoor: "The Brief 'Star Wars' Guide to International Politics," *The Washington Post*, December 17, 2015. Or as Abraham Riesman pithily puts it: "[The Jedi] were more interested in maintaining the status quo while sniping at one another in their extravagant private pyramid on the surface of a glistening ecumenopolis." Abraham Riesman: *"The Last Jedi* Is the Most Populist *Star Wars* Movie Yet," *Vulture*, December 15, 2017.

41. Hannah Arendt: *Totalitarianism: Part Three of The Origins of Totalitarianism* (San Diego, New York and London: Harvest, 1985/1968), p 10.

42. Mark Eldridge: "The Quick and Easy Path: Politics and the Force," *Eleven-ThirtyEight*, May 23, 2016.

Episode IV: "The Death Star Will Be in Range in Five Minutes"

1. Just as the Empire emerged from within the Republic, so did the Death Star, reinforcing the new left/*Star Wars* critique of the militarism of the United States. The idea of a massive planet-killing battle station dated back millennia to the Old Sith Empire, but the project originated on the planet Geonosis. The plans for what the Geonosians dubbed the "Ultimate Weapon" were given to Count Dooku, the leader of the Confederacy of Independent Systems but secretly the Sith Lord Darth Tyranus. His Master, Sheev Palpatine/ Darth Sidious, then used the story that the Separatists were building their own superweapon to frighten Republic officials into granting him funding to create the station in secret.

2. The official designation of the first Death Star was the DS-1 Orbital Battle Station. The number indicates that the original plan was never just for one station but for many. The second Death Star was

a third bigger than the original, and Starkiller Base was a converted small planet.

3. In the saga this philosophy of fear is known as the Tarkin Doctrine.

4. Oxfam: *5 Shocking Facts About Extreme Global Inequality and How to Even It Up*, undated. Further, 880 million people, more than one in eight people in the world, live in slums. This could reach 2 billion by 2030 and 3 billion by 2050.

5. NGO KnowTheChain has developed a scoring system to identify how large, global apparel and footwear companies treat workers. Despite pressure to improve conditions, the average score out of 100 remains low, at 37. KnowTheChain: *2018 Apparel & Footwear Benchmark Findings Report* (San Francisco: KnowTheChain, 2018).

6. McKinsey Global Institute: *Poorer Than Their Parents? Flat or Falling Incomes in Advanced Economies* (New York: McKinsey Global Institute, 2016).

7. Stephen Armstrong: *The New Poverty* (London: Verso, 2017).

8. Jacob S. Hacker: *The Great Risk Shift: The New Economic Insecurity and the Decline of the American Dream* (Oxford: Oxford University Press, 2008).

9. Anne Case and Angus Deaton: "Rising Morbidity and Mortality Among White Non-Hispanic Americans in the 21st Century," *Proceedings of the National Academy of Sciences of the United States of America* 112 (49), 2015.

10. Robert J. Gordon: *The Rise and Fall of American Growth: The US Standard of Living Since the Civil War* (Princeton: Princeton University Press, 2016).

11. McKinsey Global Institute: *Poorer Than Their Parents? Flat or Falling Incomes in Advanced Economies* (New York: McKinsey Global Institute, 2016).

12. Henrik Braconier, Giuseppe Nicoletti and Ben Westmore: *Policy Challenges for the Next 50 Years* (Paris: OECD, 2014).

13. International Monetary Fund: *Fiscal Monitor, Debt Use It Wisely* (Washington DC: International Monetary Fund, 2016).

14. Canaan Perry: "Conceptualisations of History in George Lucas'

'Star Wars' Saga," *space zoetrope*, June 27, 2007.

15. For example, see Martin Ford: *Rise of the Robots: Technology and the Threat of a Jobless Future* (New York: Basic Books, 2016); Martin Ford: *The Lights in the Tunnel: Automation, Accelerating Technology and the Economy of the Future* (Seattle: CreateSpace Independent Publishing Platform, 2009).

16. Carl Frey Benedikt and Michael A. Osborne: *From Brawn to Brains: The Impact of Technology on Jobs in the UK* (London: Deloitte, 2015). A study using the same methodology found that between 50 and 60 percent of jobs in most European countries could be taken over by robots or algorithms; Jeremy Bowles: *Chart of the Week: 54% of EU Jobs at Risk of Computerisation* (Brussels: Brugel, 2014).

17. McKinsey Global Institute: *Jobs Lost, Jobs Gained: Workforce Transitions in a Time of Automation* (New York: McKinsey Global Institute, 2017).

18. Randall Collins: *Technological Displacement and Capitalist Crises: Escapes and Dead Ends*, Plenary address to the Hundredth Anniversary Sociological Review Conference, Billesley Manor, UK, June 2009; Randall Collins: *The End of Middle-Class Work: No More Escapes*, p 37-70, in Immanuel Wallerstein, Randall Collins, Michael Mann, Georgi Derluguian, and Craig Calhoun: *Does Capitalism Have a Future?* (Oxford: Oxford University Press, 2013).

19. Peter Vogel: *Generation Jobless? Turning the Youth Unemployment Crisis into Opportunity* (Basingstoke: Palgrave Macmillan, 2015).

20. Kristen Bialik and Richard Fry: *Millennial Life: How Young Adulthood Today Compares with Prior Generations*, Pew Research Center, February 14, 2019.

21. Drew Desilver: *For Most US Workers, Real Wages Have Barely Budged in Decades*, Pew Research Center, August 7, 2018.

22. Center for Retirement Research at Boston College: *National Retirement Risk Index* (Boston: Center for Retirement Research at Boston College, undated).

23. Nick Srnicek: *Platform Capitalism* (Cambridge: Polity, 2016).

24. Shoshana Zuboff: *The Age of Surveillance Capitalism: The Fight for a*

Human Future at the New Frontier of Power (New York: PublicAffairs, 2019).

25. Kurt Wagner and Theodore Schleifer: "On Election Day, The Cambridge Analytica Whistleblower Is Blasting Facebook For Still Not Doing Enough," *Recode*, November 6, 2018.

26. Freedom House: *Freedom in the World 2018, Democracy in Crisis* (Washington DC: Freedom House, 2018).

27. Reporters Without Borders: *Press Freedom Index* (Paris: Reporters Without Borders, 2018).

28. OECD: *Government at a Glance 2017* (Paris: OECD Publishing, 2017).

29. Pew Research Center: *Public Trust in Government: 1958-2017* (Washington DC: Pew Research Center, 2017).

30. Harvard University Institute of Politics: *Survey of Young Americans' Attitudes toward Politics and Public Service 35th Edition: March 8 – March 25, 2018* (Cambridge, MA: Harvard University Institute of Politics).

31. Harvard University Institute of Politics: *Survey of Young Americans' Attitudes toward Politics and Public Service 33rd Edition: March 10 – March 24, 2017* (Cambridge, MA: Harvard University Institute of Politics).

32. OECD: *Trust and Public Policy, How Better Governance Can Help Rebuild Public Trust* (Paris: OECD Publishing, 2017).

33. Robert Andersen: "Support for Democracy in Cross-national Perspective: The Detrimental Effect of Economic Inequality," *Research in Social Stratification and Mobility* 30 (4), 2012, p 389-402.

34. Eric D. Gould and Alexander Hijzen: *Growing Apart, Losing Trust? The Impact of Inequality on Social Capital*, IMF Working Papers No. 16/176 (Washington DC: International Monetary Fund, 2016).

35. Johan Rockström, Will Steffen, Kevin Noone, Åsa Persson, F. Stuart III Chapin, Eric Lambin, Timothy M. Lenton, Marten Scheffer, Carl Folke, Schellnhuber Hans Joachim, Björn Nykvist, Cynthia A. de Wit, Terry Hughes, Sander van der Leeuw, Henning Rodhe, Sverker Sörlin, Peter K. Snyder, Robert Costanza, Uno Svedin, Malin Falkenmark, Louise Karlberg, Robert W. Corell, Victoria J.

Fabry, James Hansen, Brian Walker, Diana Liverman, Katherine Richardson, Paul Crutzen, and Jonathan Foley: "Planetary Boundaries: Exploring the Safe Operating Space for Humanity," *Ecology and Society* 14 (2), 2009, p 32.

36. Will Steffen, Katherine Richardson, Johan Rockström, Sarah E. Cornell, Ingo Fetzer, Elena M. Bennett, Reinette Biggs, Stephen R. Carpenter, Wim de Vries, Cynthia A. de Wit, Carl Folke, Gerten, Heinke Dieter, Georgina M. Mace Jens, Linn M. Persson, Veerabhadran Ramanathan, Belinda Reyers, and Sverker Sörlin: "Planetary Boundaries: Guiding Human Development on a Changing Planet," *Science* 347 (6223), 2015.

37. Elizabeth Kolbert: *The Sixth Extinction: An Unnatural History* (New York: Henry Holt and Company, 2014).

38. Food and Agriculture Organization of the United Nations: *How to Feed the World in 2050* (Rome: FAO, 2009).

39. United Nations Convention to Combat Desertification: *Global Land Outlook, First Edition* (Bonn: United Nations Convention to Combat Desertification, 2017).

40. Maggie Black, and Jannet King: *The Atlas of Water* (London: Earthscan Books, 2004).

41. David King, Daniel Schrag, Zhou Dadi, Qi Ye, and Arunabha Ghosh: *Climate Change, A Risk Assessment* (Cambridge: Centre for Science and Policy, University of Cambridge, 2015).

42. Christian Parenti: *Tropic of Chaos: Climate Change and the New Geography of Violence* (New York: Nation Books, 2011).

43. James Howard Kunstler: *The Long Emergency: Surviving the Converging Catastrophes of the Twenty-first Century* (New York: Grove/Atlantic, 2005).

44. The Sith Code: "Peace is a lie, there is only passion. Through passion, I gain strength. Through strength, I gain power. Through power, I gain victory. Through victory, my chains are broken. The Force shall free me." The code was created by David Gaider, who wrote part of the 2003 video game *Star Wars: Knights of the Old Republic.* Gaider reversed the Jedi Code and complemented it with

a philosophy partly inspired by Mein Kampf.

45. Charles Eisenstein: *Climate, A New Story* (Berkeley: North Atlantic Books, 2018), p 8.

46. Rebecca Solnit: "Why Climate Action Is the Antithesis of White Supremacy," *The Guardian*, 19 March 2019. Low-income nations are likely to bear 75-80 percent of the costs brought about by climate change; World Bank: *World Development Report 2010, Development and Climate Change* (Washington DC: World Bank, 2010). This is why, as Rob Nixon has said, climate change and environmental degradation represent a "slow violence" against the poor; Rob Nixon: *Slow Violence and the Environmentalism of the Poor* (Cambridge, MA: Harvard University Press, 2013).

47. Charles Derber: *Welcome to the Revolution: Universalizing Resistance for Social Justice and Democracy in Perilous Times* (New York: Routledge, 2017).

48. Denis Wood: "The Stars in Our Hearts – A Critical Commentary on George Lucas' Star Wars," *Journal of Popular Film*, 6 (3), pp 262-279.

49. Yuval Noah Harari: *21 Lessons for the 21st Century* (London: Jonathan Cape, 2018), p 16.

50. As described by Ian Lowrie: "On Algorithmic Communism," *Los Angeles Review of Books*, January 8, 2018.

51. As George Lucas put it: "[T]his idea of democracy being given up... in a time of crisis; you see it throughout history whether it's Julius Caesar or Napoleon or Adolf Hitler. You see these democracies under a lot of pressure...in a crisis situation who end up giving up a lot of the freedoms they have and a lot of the checks and balances to somebody with a strong authority to help get them through the crisis..." Audio commentary to *Star Wars Episode II: Attack of the Clones* (DVD, Lucasfilm, 2002).

52. Naomi Klein: *The Shock Doctrine: The Rise of Disaster Capitalism* (New York: Picador 2008).

53. Naomi, Oreskes and Erik M. Conway: *The Collapse of Western Civilization: A View from the Future* (New York: Columbia University Press, 2014).

54. As noted by Robert Kuttner: *Can Democracy Survive Global Capitalism?* (New York: W. W. Norton & Company, 2018).

55. The Separatist movement in the *Star Wars* prequels captures the authoritarian-populist coalition rather well: corporations who want to escape taxes and regulation at the top, and a frustrated populace who've lost faith in the Republic at the bottom. For an excellent analysis, see Mohammed Shakibnia: "What The Clone Wars Can Teach Us About Racial, Social, and Economic Justice," *Eleven-ThirtyEight*, February 4, 2019.

56. Antonio Negri: "A 21st Century Fascist," Verso blog, January 16, 2019.

57. Peter Frase: *Four Futures, Life After Capitalism* (London: Verso, 2016).

58. Wolfgang Streeck: *How Will Capitalism End? Essays on a Failing System* (London: Verso, 2016).

59. Anxiety and Depression Association of America: *Facts & Statistics*, undated.

60. Laura-Jane Rawlings: *Latest Research: Young People Fear for Their Emotional Health*, The Prince's Trust Macquarie Youth Index, April 6, 2018.

61. Robert Booth: "Anxiety on Rise Among the Young in Social Media Age," *The Guardian*, February 5, 2019.

62. Sally Weale: "UK Second Only to Japan For Young People's Poor Mental Wellbeing," *The Guardian*, February 8, 2017.

63. Shoshana Zuboff: *The Age of Surveillance Capitalism: The Fight for a Human Future at the New Frontier of Power* (New York: PublicAffairs, 2019).

64. Dave Schilling: "Star Wars: The Last Jedi Review: The Star Wars Film That Finally Lives Up To Empire Strikes Back," *Birth.Movies. Death*, December 12, 2017. Explaining his motivation playing a disenchanted Luke in *The Last Jedi*, Mark Hamill similarly explained that: "I was eleven when the Beatles hit and they were the peace and love generation, and when I was in high school…I believed all that. I thought by the time we get in power they'll be no more wars.

We'll end world famine...[But] we failed!...Thought Watergate was bad? That was just two parties. Now it's a political entity with a hostile foreign government and...we've been in perpetual war." Alex Leadbeater: "Mark Hamill Draws from Real-Life Politics for Luke Skywalker's Darkness," *Screen Rant*, December 5, 2017.

65. For example, Susan Hatters-Friedman and Ryan C. W. Hall, a pair of psychiatrist-professors, use the movies to illustrate the causes and complexity of various conditions: Susan Hatters-Friedman and Ryan C. W. Hall: "Teaching Psychopathology in a Galaxy Far, Far Away: The Light Side of the Force," *Academic Psychiatry*, December 2015, pp 719-725; Susan Hatters-Friedman and Ryan C. W. Hall: "Psychopathology in a Galaxy Far, Far Away: The Use of Star Wars' Dark Side in Teaching," *Academic Psychiatry*, 39 (6), December 2015, pp 726-732.

66. Michael Sragow: "Universal Themes," *The Baltimore Sun*, May 16, 2012.

67. Martin Winiecki: "80 Years Since the Holocaust Began: Can We Stop Fascism Today?," *Common Dreams*, November 10, 2018.

68. As quoted in Richard Corliss and Jess Cagle: "Dark Victory," *Time*, April 29, 2002.

69. Eva Wiseman: "Ellen Page: I'm Not Afraid to Say the Truth," *The Guardian*, January 20, 2019.

70. Michael J. Hanson and Max S. Kay: *Star Wars: The New Myth* (Bloomington: Xlibris, 2002), p 32.

Episode V: "That's How We're Gonna Win. Not Fighting What We Hate, but Saving What We Love"

1. Lawyer and conservative blogger Gray Connolly argues that: "The Rebels were little more than the far ago galaxy's version of the Weather Underground, attention-seeking, indulged poseurs, addicted to violent and often lethal attacks on lawful authority. The dissolution of the Empire and its replacement by a pre-modern anarchy of hippy Ewoks dancing around the ruins of the imperial project was never voted for by any imperial subject. For all of

Leia, Luke, Han and the other ne'er-do-wells' bravado and talk of 'Freedom', they never trusted 'the People' they so loudly claimed to represent." Gray Connolly: "Star Wars: The Realist Case for the Empire," *Strategy Counsel*, November 6, 2015.

2. Mike Lux, *How to Democrat in the Age Of Trump* (Washington DC: Strong Arm Press, 2018).

3. Kate Aronoff: "Star Wars: The Last Jedi Takes a Side in the Class War," *The Intercept*, December 24, 2017.

4. Potter didn't actually name the system, whether imperialism or capitalism, perhaps because this would have distracted from its message for a broader audience, but also because it was for the movement to name it, not just one individual.

5. Paul Potter: "The Incredible War: Speech at the Washington Antiwar March (April 17, 1965)," in Massimo Teodori (ed), *The New Left: A Documentary History* (New York: Bobbs-Merrill, 1968), p 246-248.

6. Mike Konczal and Nell Abernathy: "Democrats Must Become the Party of Freedom," *Talking Points Memo*, November 1, 2018.

7. Mike Lux: *How to Democrat in the Age of Trump* (Washington DC: Strong Arm Press, 2018).

8. Chantal Mouffe: *For a Left Populism* (London: Verso, 2018).

9. As quoted in Irving Howe (ed): *A Margin of Hope: An Intellectual Autobiography* (New York: Harcourt Brace, 1982), p 132-133.

10. Robert Kuttner: "Comment: Why Liberals Need Radicals," *The American Prospect*, December 19, 2001.

11. Jane Mayer: *Dark Money: The Hidden History of the Billionaires Behind the Rise of the Radical Right* (New York: Anchor Books, 2017).

12. Eric Gellner: "Corruption, Exploitation, and Decay: The Politics of Star Wars," *Star Wars*, November 6, 2012.

13. The animated *The Clone Wars* TV series portrays Padmé with more political agency. She defends democracy in amidst a corrupt Senate and mounting fear and radicalization as she tries to advocate for ordinary people.

14. As told in *The Clone Wars*, others also try to respond to the

emergency with normal democratic measures, not realizing the nature of the threat. Concerned with Palpatine's growing lust for power as the war progresses, Bail Organa and Mon Mothma formed the Delegation of 2000 to petition Palpatine to stop amending the constitution to remain in power. But there would be no forcing him to restore the Republic to its pre-war state; after wiping out the Jedi with his Order 66, Palpatine called a special session of the Senate in which he claimed a Jedi assassination attempt on his life and declared himself Emperor of the first Galactic Empire.

15. Becky Sharp: "Star Wars Politics Part Two: The Right Side Strikes Back," *Retrozap*. November 7, 2016.

16. Robert Kuttner: "Comment: Why Liberals Need Radicals," *The American Prospect*, December 19, 2001.

17. Charles Eisenstein: *Climate, A New Story* (Berkeley: North Atlantic Books, 2018).

18. Jeff Gomez: "Story Can Assert Control Over the Masses," *Collective Journey*, Medium, February 27, 2017.

19. Fred Polak: *The Image of the Future* (London: Elsevier Scientific Publishing Company, 1973).

20. Wes Bishop: "Where We Build Our Rebellions: Review Of 'Rogue One' and the Political Ethics of Star Wars," *Tersejournal*, January 18, 2017.

21. Charles Derber: *Welcome to the Revolution: Universalizing Resistance for Social Justice and Democracy in Perilous Times* (New York: Routledge, 2017).

22. Laurence Cox: "How Events in 1968 Reshaped the World," *New Frame*, January 21, 2019.

23. Andrew Gamble: *Open Left: The Future of Progressive Politics* (London: Rowman & Littlefield International, 2018).

24. Denis Wood: "The Stars in Our Hearts – A Critical Commentary on George Lucas' Star Wars," *Journal of Popular Film*, 6 (3), pp 262-279.

25. Angry Staff Officer: "In The Last Jedi, The Resistance Keeps Making the Same Tactical Mistake," *Wired*, December 19, 2017.

26. Zachary Feinstein: *It's a Trap: Emperor Palpatine's Poison Pill,*

Washington University in St. Louis, December 1, 2015.

27. Zachary Feinstein: *It's a Trap: Emperor Palpatine's Poison Pill*, Washington University in St. Louis, December 1, 2015, p 9.

28. Rebecca Solnit: "'Hope Is an Embrace of The Unknown': Rebecca Solnit On Living in Dark Times," *Rebecca Solnit*, July 15, 2016.

29. *Žižek on Reshooting Star Wars (funny)*, https://www.youtube.com/watch?v=T_DroaGggbc

30. "When I say the only change is that the left appropriates fascism and so on, it's not a cheap joke. The point is to avoid the trap of standard liberal oppositions: freedom versus totalitarian order, and so on, to rehabilitate notions of discipline, collective order, subordination, sacrifice, all that. I don't think this is inherently fascist." *Slavoj Žižek's House, Stalin Poster, and Weird Kitchen* https://www.youtube.com/watch?v=JA60L_NQYm0&feature=youtu.be

31. Jodi Dean: *Democracy and Other Neoliberal Fantasies* (Durham: Duke University Press, 2009); *The Communist Horizon* (London: Verso, October 2012).

32. Nicos Poulantzas: *State, Power, Socialism* (London: Verso, 1978). Marx also believed in a democratic republic: popular control of the state, universal suffrage, representative democracy, a democratic constitution and mass involvement in political decision-making. Hal Draper: *Karl Marx's Theory of Revolution. Volume III The "Dictatorship of the Proletariat"* (New York: Monthly Review Press, 1986); *The "Dictatorship of the Proletariat" from Marx to Lenin* (New York: Monthly Review Press, 1987).

33. Alan Johnson: "Slavoj Žižek's Theory of Revolution: A Critique," chapter three, in Matthew Johnson (ed): *The Legacy of Marxism: Contemporary Challenges, Conflicts, and Developments* (London: Continuum, 2012).

34. *Clerks*, Miramax, 1994.

35. As Adam Kirsch argues: "There is a name for the politics that glorifies risk, decision, and will; that yearns for the hero, the master, and the leader; that prefers death and the infinite to democracy and the pragmatic; that finds the only true freedom in the terror of

violence. Its name is not communism." Adam Kirsch: "The Deadly Jester," *New Republic*, December 2, 2008.

36. Erica Chenoweth and Maria Stephan: *Why Civil Resistance Works: The Strategic Logic of Nonviolent Conflict* (New York: Columbia University Press, 2013).

37. Howard Ryan: *Critique of Nonviolent Politics: From Mahatma Gandhi to the Anti-Nuclear Movement* (2002).

38. Discussions of *Star Wars* and Eastern philosophy can be found in Kevin S. Decker and Jason T. Eberl (eds): *Star Wars and Philosophy: More Powerful Than You Can Possibly Imagine* (Chicago and La Salle: Open Court, 2005), and Matthew Bortolin: *The Dharma of Star Wars* (Somerville: Wisdom Publications, 2015), among others.

39. To Cass Sunstein, the first six films are about parents and redemption, Cass R. Sunstein: *The World According to Star Wars* (New York: HarperCollins, 2016). Douglas Williams similarly suggests that: "Though there are many films about the conflict between parents and children in the 60s and 70s that present conflict...no film in the late 60s and 70s...showed a narrative of reconciliation – nor could it...But the Star Wars films do have that conflict...In these films, the child redeems the parent...and the world is healed." Douglas Williams: "Not So Long Ago and Far Away: Star Wars, Republics and Empires of Tomorrow," p 229-353, in Gregg Rickman (ed): *The Science Fiction Film Reader* (New York: Limelight Press, 2004).

40. Mark Eldridge: "How We Choose to Fight – War and the Force," *Eleven-ThirtyEight*, November 27, 2017.

41. Arundhati Roy: "Confronting Empire," p 103-112, in *War Talk* (Cambridge: South End Press, 2003).

Episode VI: "There Has Been an Awakening. Have You Felt It?"

1. In saga lore, it's more conspiratorial. According to Wookieepedia, the Rebel Alliance's formation was secretly instigated by the Sith. In a plot for drawing the Emperor's enemies out from hiding, Darth Vader ordered his secret apprentice, Starkiller, to organize

dissidents into a large resistance movement. After Starkiller was betrayed by his master however, the former apprentice sacrificed himself to ensure the survival of the Rebel leaders. When the Alliance to Restore the Republic was officially formed, the Rebels honored his memory by basing their organization's emblem on the Marek family crest, turning it into a symbol of hope.

2. Mikkel Bolt Rasmussen makes a related point, that in attempting to fuse popular culture and ultra-nationalism to renew the old alliance between the white working class and the capitalist class, Trump's late-capitalist fascism is the latest backlash against the new new left, preventing the coming into being of an anti-capitalist alliance between Occupy and Black Lives Matter. Mikkel Bolt Rasmussen: *Trump's Counter-Revolution* (London: Zero Books, 2018).

3. Amy Erica Smith: "Solo Reveals the Weakness of The Star Wars Galactic Empire," *Vox*, June 20, 2018.

4. For a fascinating book of Imperial and Rebel propaganda posters, see Pablo Hidalgo: *Star Wars Propaganda: A History of Persuasive Art in the Galaxy* (New York: Harper Design, 2016).

5. Jennifer Gidley: *The Future: A Very Short Introduction* (Oxford: Oxford University Press, 2017), p 2.

6. Joseph Campbell and Bill Moyers: *The Power of Myth* (New York: Anchor Books, 1991), p xiv.

7. Mark Fisher: *Capitalist Realism: Is There No Alternative?* (London: Zero Books, 2009), p 15.

8. Václav Havel: *New Year's Address to the Nation*, speech, January 1, 1990.

9. Bill Moyers: *Joseph Campbell and the Power of Myth, Episode 1: The Hero's Adventure*, June 21, 1988.

10. Wes Bishop: "Where We Build Our Rebellions: Review Of 'Rogue One' and the Political Ethics of Star Wars," *Tersejournal*, January 18, 2017.

11. Chris Crass: "Lessons from the Rebel Alliance on the 40th Anniversary of Star Wars," *Medium*, May 25, 2017.

12. Quoted in Matthew Kapell and John Shelton Lawrence (eds):

Finding the Force of the Star Wars Franchise: Fans, Merchandise, & Critics (New York: Peter Lang, 2006), p 44.

13. TEDxYouth@SanDiego: *Orphans vs. Empires: Andrew Slack at TEDxYouth@SanDiego (2013)*, TED. https://www.youtube.com/watch?v=pQYvliWUfng

14. James Martin: *The Meaning of the 21st Century: A Vital Blueprint for Ensuring Our Future* (New York: Riverhead Books, 2006), p 7. Neil Howe and William Strauss make a similar point in one of their generational studies. They view millennials as a generation that "is going to rebel by behaving not worse, but better...For Millennials, this shift will focus on the needs of the community more than the individual, it is likely to induce large-scale institutional change. Thus, the word *rebellion* is not entirely appropriate. The word *revolution* might better capture the spirit of what lies ahead." Neil Howe and William Strauss: *Millennials Rising: The Next Great Generation* (New York: Vintage Books, 2000), p 7, 67.

15. But a great place to start is Greg Jobin-Leeds and AgitArte: *When We Fight, We Win: Twenty-First-Century Social Movements and the Activists That Are Transforming Our World* (New York: The New Press, 2016).

16. BLM is not just about protest. In 2015 Johnetta Elzie, DeRay Mckesson, Brittany Packnett and Samuel Sinyangwe launched Campaign Zero, aimed at promoting policy reforms to end police brutality. The campaign released a ten-point plan for reforms to policing, with recommendations including ending broken windows policing, increasing community oversight of police departments and creating stricter guidelines for the use of force.

17. As David Hogg, one of the survivors and leaders of the movement, recalls thinking when the shooting was still happening: "'Am I going to be just another background character? Is this what it's all been leading up to? Just a bullet to the head?' And I decided, 'Okay, I may be another background character, but if I'm going to die I'm going to die telling a damn good story that people need to hear,'" David Hogg and Lauren Hogg: *#NeverAgain, A New*

Generation Draws The Line (New York: Random House: 2018), p 4.

18. Estimates suggest that between one and half to two million people marched that day, making it the third or fourth largest 1-day protest in American history, equivalent to the largest protest of the Vietnam War era.

19. The biggest was the Global Climate March which took place in cities around the world on 29th November 2015, the day before the opening of the United Nations Climate Change Conference in Paris. An estimated 785,000 people took part in more than 2000 events in 175 countries. Less than a year earlier, more than 310,000 had marched in New York City and a similar number around the world as part of the People's Climate March. A second People's Climate March took place in April 2017 on the National Mall in Washington DC, 300 locations throughout the US, and across the world, to protest the environmental policies of the newly-elected President Donald Trump and his administration.

20. As the students state: "We are the voiceless future of humanity. We will no longer accept this injustice. We demand justice for all past, current and future victims of the climate crisis, and so we are rising up...We will not accept a life in fear and devastation. We have the right to live our dreams and hopes...We, the young, have started to move. We are going to change the fate of humanity, whether you like it or not." The Global Coordination Group of The Youth-Led Climate Strike: "Climate Crisis and a Betrayed Generation," letter, *The Guardian*, March 1, 2019.

21. Mark Engler and Paul Engler: *This Is an Uprising: How Nonviolent Revolt Is Shaping the Twenty-First Century* (New York: Nation Books, 2016).

22. Doyle Canning and Patrick Reinsborough: *Re:Imagining Change: How to Use Story-Based Strategy to Win Campaigns, Build Movements, and Change the World* (Oakland: PM Press, 2017).

23. Henry Jenkins, Sangita Shresthova, Liana Gamber-Thompson, Neta Kligler-Vilenchik, Arely Zimmerman: *By Any Media Necessary, The New Youth Activism* (New York: New York University Press, 2016).

Endnotes

24. Sujatha Fernandes: *Curated Stories: The Uses and Misuses of Storytelling* (Oxford: Oxford University Press, 2017).
25. Sujatha Fernandes: *Curated Stories: The Uses and Misuses of Storytelling* (Oxford: Oxford University Press, 2017), Foreword.
26. Charles Derber: *Welcome to the Revolution: Universalizing Resistance for Social Justice and Democracy in Perilous Times* (New York: Routledge, 2017).
27. George Lakey: *How We Win, A Guide to Nonviolent Direct Action Campaigning* (New York: Melville House Publishing, 2018).
28. Paul Mason: *Why It's Kicking Off Everywhere* (London: Verso Books, 2012). See also Alan Sears: *The Next New Left: A History of the Future* (Nova Scotia: Fernwood Publishing, 2014).
29. Jonathan Smucker: *Hegemony How-To: A Roadmap for Radicals* (Chico: AK Press, 2017). See also Zeynep Tufekci: *Twitter and Teargas: The Power and Fragility of Networked Protest* (New Haven: Yale University Press, 2017). Like Smucker, Tufekci warns against the new new left's distrust of formal leadership, which means they run into a "tactical freeze" – an inability to adjust tactics, negotiate demands and push for tangible policy changes.
30. Nick Srnicek and Alex Williams: *Inventing the Future: Postcapitalism and a World Without Work* (London: Verso, 2015).
31. Micah White: *The End of Protest: A New Playbook for Revolution* (Toronto: Knopf Canada, 2016).
32. Kate Aronoff: "'Star Wars: The Last Jedi' Takes a Side in the Class War," *The Intercept*, December 24, 2017.
33. Kate Aronoff, Alyssa Battistoni, Daniel Aldana Cohen, and Thea Riofrancos: "The Green New Deal's Five Freedoms," *Jacobin*, February 6, 2019.
34. Wes Bishop: "Where We Build Our Rebellions: Review Of 'Rogue One' and the Political Ethics of Star Wars," *Tersejournal*, January 18, 2017.
35. As Lucas intimates: "All of Star Wars is reasonably political... sometimes the politics are confused and muddled in terms of the way people see it which is the way most people see politics but it

is because people are confused and muddled people don't want to have anything to do with it. Of course, if they don't want anything to do with it that's why they end up turning to somebody to take over and clean it all up." Audio commentary to *Star Wars Episode III: Revenge of the Sith* (DVD, Lucasfilm, 2005).

36. *George Lucas – Be Compassionate.* https://www.goalcast.com/2017/01/06/georges-lucas-choose-your-path/

37. Speaking about *American Graffiti*, Lucas reflected: "All [THX] did was make people more pessimistic, more depressed, and less willing to get involved in trying to make the world better. So I decided that this time I would make a more optimistic film that makes people feel positive about their fellow human beings. It's too easy to make films about Watergate. And it's hard to be optimistic when everything tells you to be pessimistic and cynical. I'm a very bad cynic. But we've got to regenerate optimism." As quoted in Sally Kline (ed): *George Lucas: Interviews* (Jackson: University Press of Mississippi, 1999), p 42.

38. John Powers: "Last Thoughts on Episode VII: Quasi Infinities and The Waning of The Force," *Star Wars Modern*, December 26, 2012.

39. Rebecca Solnit: *Hope in the Dark: Untold Histories, Wild Possibilities* (London: Canongate, 2016).

40. As Mark Fisher wrote: "In particularly acute cases of depression... [t]he only effective remedy is to do things, even though the patient will, at that time, believe that any act is pointless and meaningless. But 'going through the motions' of the act is an essential pre-requisite to the growth of belief 'in the heart'...[B]elief follows from behavior rather than the reverse. Similarly, the only way out of cultural depression like now is to act as if things can be different." Mark Fisher: "Optimism of the Act," *k-punk*, February 24, 2006.

41. Václav Havel: *Disturbing the Peace: A Conversation with Karel Huizdala* (New York: Vintage Books, 1991), p 182.

42. As Chuck Wendig notes, this scene speaks to new fans and potential rebels: "This storyworld has long been generational:

each generation now getting a trilogy for them, unique to them, and this is that, here...[It] remake[s] it for kids my son's age...kids who don't have to look like Luke Skywalker but can instead look like Rose or Finn or Poe or Rey." Chuck Wendig: "The Last Jedi: A Mirror Slowly Cracking," *Chuck Wendig: TerribleMinds*, December 18, 2017.

43. The ring was an antique from the galactic civil war, used by members of the Imperial Senate to secretly signal their allegiance to the Rebellion. The ring was given to Rose by her commanding officer in memory of her sister Paige, so it means something for her to hand it on.

Epilogue: "The Rebellion Is Reborn Today"

1. Denis Wood: "The Stars in Our Hearts – A Critical Commentary on George Lucas' Star Wars," *Journal of Popular Film*, 6 (3), pp 262-279.

"Hello There"

Thank you for buying *Welcome to the Rebellion*.

To be honest, I never expected to write a book about politics and *Star Wars*. As I say in the book, I was certainly a young fan of the saga. *A New Hope* was the first film I saw at the cinema, and it represented a whole new world. At the same cinema a few years later, I watched all three of the Original Trilogy films back-to-back (me and a friend smuggled in lunchboxes). I only returned to watching a *Star Wars* film at the flicks with the release of *Revenge of the Sith*. I thought what we then expected to be the conclusion of the saga deserved the price of a ticket. Yes, there were rumors when we were kids that there were eventually meant to be six or nine films, which was kind of mind-blowing, but after *The Return of the Jedi* everything went quiet... *Star Wars* seemed to be at an end.

Of course, it would come back, but not so much for me. After studying politics at university, I became a researcher, moving around different organizations every few years. I've been lucky enough to work in lots of different areas, from education and technology, to innovation, government, public services and urban planning.

Strangely, *Welcome to the Rebellion* comes out of the first book I wrote, called *A Future for Planning: Taking Responsibility for Twenty-First Century Challenges* (Routledge, 2019). As the title suggests, that book was about the big challenges we face in this century, from climate change and demographic change, to automation and artificial intelligence, political instability and systemic risk. It made me think, if our politicians aren't preparing us for these problems, where is the book that tells young people how they might navigate a very different future?

I might still write that book, but whenever I mentioned the idea to people, they'd express some skepticism. Sure, they could see how it was needed, but wouldn't it be really depressing (which is to say, did I think anyone would buy it?). That made me think about the importance of hope, and the need for stories to promote a new sense of hope among young people...and so here we are.

This book was written before the release of *The Rise of Skywalker*, so accept my apologies for not being able to provide any perspective on the totality of the saga and how this might affect any of the points made here. What seems certain, however, is that *Star Wars* will continue to draw on contemporary political themes and issues for a new generation of fans. Given the argument made in this book, how could it not?

If you have a few moments, do leave a review (whether you liked the book or not) on the usual book-selling sites. I'd really appreciate it. And if you'd be interested in hearing about forthcoming books, do visit my own site at: www. drmichaeljharrisbooks.com

So, that's it. As a hero once said, "You're all clear, kid! Now let's blow this thing and go home!"

ZERO
BOOKS

CULTURE, SOCIETY & POLITICS

Contemporary culture has eliminated the concept and public figure of the intellectual. A cretinous anti-intellectualism presides, cheer-led by hacks in the pay of multinational corporations who reassure their bored readers that there is no need to rouse themselves from their stupor. Zer0 Books knows that another kind of discourse – intellectual without being academic, popular without being populist – is not only possible: it is already flourishing. Zer0 is convinced that in the unthinking, blandly consensual culture in which we live, critical and engaged theoretical reflection is more important than ever before.

If you have enjoyed this book, why not tell other readers by posting a review on your preferred book site.

Recent bestsellers from Zero Books are:

In the Dust of This Planet
Horror of Philosophy vol. 1
Eugene Thacker
In the first of a series of three books on the Horror of Philosophy,
In the Dust of This Planet offers the genre of horror as a way of
thinking about the unthinkable.
Paperback: 978-1-84694-676-9 ebook: 978-1-78099-010-1

Capitalist Realism
Is there no alternative?
Mark Fisher
An analysis of the ways in which capitalism has presented itself
as the only realistic political-economic system.
Paperback: 978-1-84694-317-1 ebook: 978-1-78099-734-6

Rebel Rebel
Chris O'Leary
David Bowie: every single song. Everything you want to know,
everything you didn't know.
Paperback: 978-1-78099-244-0 ebook: 978-1-78099-713-1

Cartographies of the Absolute
Alberto Toscano, Jeff Kinkle
An aesthetics of the economy for the twenty-first century.
Paperback: 978-1-78099-275-4 ebook: 978-1-78279-973-3

Romeo and Juliet in Palestine
Teaching Under Occupation
Tom Sperlinger
Life in the West Bank, the nature of pedagogy and the role of a
university under occupation.
Paperback: 978-1-78279-637-4 ebook: 978-1-78279-636-7

Malign Velocities
Accelerationism and Capitalism
Benjamin Noys
Long listed for the Bread and Roses Prize 2015, *Malign
Velocities* argues against the need for speed, tracking acceleration
as the symptom of the ongoing crises of capitalism.
Paperback: 978-1-78279-300-7 ebook: 978-1-78279-299-4

Meat Market
Female Flesh under Capitalism
Laurie Penny
A feminist dissection of women's bodies as the fleshy fulcrum of
capitalist cannibalism, whereby women are both consumers and
consumed.
Paperback: 978-1-84694-521-2 ebook: 978-1-84694-782-7

Poor but Sexy
Culture Clashes in Europe East and West
Agata Pyzik
How the East stayed East and the West stayed West.
Paperback: 978-1-78099-394-2 ebook: 978-1-78099-395-9

Sweetening the Pill
or How We Got Hooked on Hormonal Birth Control
Holly Grigg-Spall
Has contraception liberated or oppressed women? *Sweetening the Pill* breaks the silence on the dark side of hormonal contraception.
Paperback: 978-1-78099-607-3 ebook: 978-1-78099-608-0

Why Are We The Good Guys?
Reclaiming your Mind from the Delusions of Propaganda
David Cromwell
A provocative challenge to the standard ideology that Western power is a benevolent force in the world.
Paperback: 978-1-78099-365-2 ebook: 978-1-78099-366-9

Readers of ebooks can buy or view any of these bestsellers by clicking on the live link in the title. Most titles are published in paperback and as an ebook. Paperbacks are available in traditional bookshops. Both print and ebook formats are available online.
Find more titles and sign up to our readers' newsletter at http://www.johnhuntpublishing.com/culture-and-politics
Follow us on Facebook
at https://www.facebook.com/ZeroBooks
and Twitter at https://twitter.com/Zer0Books